CONTENTS

New Directions for
Child and Adolescent
Development

Lene Arnett Jensen
Reed W. Larson
EDITORS-IN-CHIEF

William Damon
FOUNDING EDITOR

Origins of Ownership of Property

Hildy Ross
Ori Friedman
EDITORS

Number 132 • Summer 2011
Jossey-Bass
San Francisco

ORIGINS OF OWNERSHIP OF PROPERTY
Hildy Ross, Ori Friedman (eds.)
New Directions for Child and Adolescent Development, no. 132
Lene Arnett Jensen, Reed W. Larson, Editors-in-Chief

Microfilm copies of issues and articles are available in 16mm and 35mm, as well as microfiche in 105mm, through University Microfilms, Inc., 300 North Zeeb Road, Ann Arbor, Michigan 48106-1346.

ISSN 1520-3247   electronic ISSN 1534-8687

NEW DIRECTIONS FOR CHILD AND ADOLESCENT DEVELOPMENT is part of The Jossey-Bass Education Series and is published quarterly by Wiley Subscription Services, Inc., a Wiley company, at Jossey-Bass, 989 Market Street, San Francisco, California 94103-1741. Periodicals postage paid at San Francisco, California, and at additional mailing offices. Postmaster: Send address changes to New Directions for Child and Adolescent Development, Jossey-Bass, 989 Market Street, San Francisco, CA 94103-1741.

New Directions for Child and Adolescent Development is indexed in Cambridge Scientific Abstracts (CSA/CIG), CHID: Combined Health Information Database (NIH), Contents Pages in Education (T&F), Current Abstracts (EBSCO), Educational Research Abstracts Online (T&F), EMBASE/Excerpta Medica (Elsevier), ERIC Database (Education Resources Information Center), Index Medicus/MEDLINE/PubMed (NLM), Linguistics & Language Behavior Abstracts (CSA/CIG), Psychological Abstracts/PsycINFO (APA), Social Services Abstracts (CSA/CIG), SocINDEX (EBSCO), and Sociological Abstracts (CSA/CIG).

SUBSCRIPTION rates: For the U.S., $89 for individuals and $315 for institutions. Please see ordering information page at end of journal.

EDITORIAL CORRESPONDENCE should be e-mailed to the editors-in-chief: Lene Arnett Jensen (ljensen@clarku.edu) and Reed W. Larson (larsonr@ illinois.edu).

Jossey-Bass Web address: www.josseybass.com

Friedman, O., & Ross, H. (2011). Twenty-one reasons to care about the psychological basis of ownership. In H. Ross & O. Friedman (Eds.), Origins of ownership of property. New Directions for Child and Adolescent Development, 132, 1–8.

1

Twenty-One Reasons to Care About the Psychological Basis of Ownership

Ori Friedman, Hildy Ross

Abstract

The psychological basis of ownership is a neglected area of research; the authors consider twenty-one disparate reasons why it is worth investigating.

NEW DIRECTIONS FOR CHILD AND ADOLESCENT DEVELOPMENT, no. 132, Summer 2011 © Wiley Periodicals, Inc.
Published online in Wiley Online Library (wileyonlinelibrary.com). • DOI: 10.1002/cd.292

1

> There is nothing which so generally strikes the imagination, and engages the affections of mankind, as the right of property; or that sole and despotic dominion which one man claims and exercises over the external things of the world, in total exclusion of the right of any other individual in the universe. And yet there are very few, that will give themselves the trouble to consider the origin and foundation of that right.
>
> William Blackstone (1766). Commentaries on the Laws of England, Book II: Of the Rights of Things (p. 2).

With these words, William Blackstone drew attention to the relative neglect of ownership in the scholarship of his times and began his own treatise on property. Since then philosophers, historians, legal scholars, biologists, and social scientists have taken up the call to analyze property rights. Within psychology, most aspects of ownership have received scant attention or have been overlooked completely. In this chapter, we outline twenty-one reasons why it will be important (and interesting) to understand the psychological basis of ownership of property, including its developmental origins.

1. *Daily life.* Ownership is involved in many common activities, including selling and buying, lending and borrowing, giving and receiving gifts, donating and begging for charity. Knowledge about ownership allows children to take part in these activities and to understand their structure and implications.

2. *A human universal, and cultural and cross-species variation.* Ownership is a human universal; property rights have been found in all human cultures (Brown, 1991). Ownership may also have existed in the prehistoric world, as can be inferred from the existence of trade routes. Hence, understanding the psychological basis of ownership may be informative about all people. At the same time, ownership may vary considerably across cultures, and so ownership provides a window for understanding cultural variation. Likewise, many animal species show possessive, ownership-like behaviors. Brosnan (this volume) reviews the evidence for and limitations of ownership behavior across animal species (also see, Stake, 2004). So ownership also provides a domain for making interspecies comparisons.

3. *Myriad inferences.* Ownership is multifaceted. In reasoning about ownership, people draw many sorts of inferences, including inferences about who can be an owner; inferences about what sorts of things can be owned; inferences about which privileges are conferred by ownership; inferences about how ownership is established, transferred, and relinquished; inferences about whether a particular object is owned; and inferences about who the owner is (Blake & Harris, this volume; Friedman, Neary, Defeyter & Malcolm, this volume; Kalish & Anderson, this volume; Noles & Keil, this volume). Presumably diverse rules and processes

NEW DIRECTIONS FOR CHILD AND ADOLESCENT DEVELOPMENT • DOI: 10.1002/cd

underlie these varied inferences. The nature of these rules and processes, and their development in children, is almost entirely unknown.

4. An abstract concept. Much work in cognitive development has investigated children's possession of abstract concepts, including mental state concepts, numerical concepts, and moral concepts. Abstract concepts do not correspond with things perceivable by the senses, and so it is mysterious how children come to acquire them. Ownership is also clearly abstract (Jackendoff, 1992). In looking at some object, it cannot be directly perceived whether it belongs to one person rather than another (or no one at all). It is also impossible to perceive the privileges that ownership confers. Hence, ownership provides another domain for studying how it is that people possess and use abstract concepts.

5. Object cognition. Most owned things are objects, and today most objects around us are owned. Reasoning about ownership, then, can be viewed as a form of object-cognition, much like considering an object's physical properties, category membership, or function. In fact, Blake and Harris (this volume) suggest that ownership is represented as an attribute of objects, and a means by which similar objects can be distinguished—for instance one might contrast two books by saying that one belongs to Anne while the other belongs to her friend Bob. By understanding ownership we better understand an important determinant of how children and adults alike relate to objects.

6. Beyond objects. Beyond inanimate physical objects, many other entities can be viewed as owned, including one's own body, land, animals, and various sorts of intellectual property (Noles & Keil, this volume; Olson & Shaw, in press; Rochat, this volume). Noles and Keil suggest that children and adults have similar intuitions about which sorts of things can be owned. Ownership reasoning may also be applied to things that are not explicitly viewed as owned. For instance, people might view their mates as property (Wilson & Daly, 1992), and perhaps the parent–child relationship also has elements of ownership. Jealousy may result from applying ownership principles to others. Even when ownership is not explicitly acknowledged, it may influence people's behavior and reasoning in many domains.

7. Behaving in relation to things. People typically consider ownership when planning behavior in relation to things. Anne can underline words in her book; she will be less likely to do this in a book borrowed from her friend Bob. As Friedman et al. (this volume) stress, before interacting with an object it is important to consider whether it is owned or not and, if it is owned, by whom. To show mature behavior in relation to objects, children must come to make such inferences about ownership.

8. Social behavior. Ownership also influences how people relate to one another. Suppose Carl takes Anne's book and (without permission) starts writing in it. Those who know that Anne is the owner (including Anne herself) will probably protest, and may try to prevent Carl from writing any more. Moreover, they will view Carl negatively for interfering with Anne's property. Ownership priorities help people avoid and resolve many social conflicts.

9. *Understanding behavior.* Reasoning about ownership is crucial for understanding and predicting behavior (Snare, 1972). Doug, a stranger to Anne, will not take Anne's book, even when she leaves it and goes to order a coffee. Understanding Doug's behavior (or lack of it) requires reasoning about ownership: Anne owns the book, so Doug should not take it. Reasoning about ownership likewise allows Doug's behavior to be predicted in advance. Reasoning about ownership is a form of social cognition.

10. *Rights and transgressions.* One reason that ownership impacts behavior is that ownership confers specific rights and privileges with respect to property. Anne's ownership of the book implies that other people are excluded from it—they *ought* not to use it (without her permission). Ross, Conant, and Vickar (this volume) provide evidence that quite young children adhere to this "right of exclusion" (see also Ross, 1996). People who violate this right are viewed as taking morally wrong, often illegal actions. These actions include theft, trespassing, and vandalism—moral transgression specific to ownership.

11. *Responsibilities of owners.* Ownership may also have further moral consequences because owners are responsible for their property. Ownership rights are constrained by other moral obligations. Although owners are typically permitted to use their property, they cannot use it to harm others. More than this, negligent owners are sometimes culpable when their property is involved in harm.

12. *Social relationships.* Ownership is moderated by social relationships. For instance, although Anne's ownership of the book strictly means that non-owners are excluded from using it (without her permission), this limitation may apply more strongly to strangers than it does to Anne's friends or to her family members. It would be socially awkward for Anne to deny ordinary access to a friend, and doing so might affect the nature of their relationship. Fiske's (1992) theory of social relations outlines how social obligations (often involving ownership, though not limited to it) vary across four types of social relations. Young children may not share their parents' appreciation that social obligations can temper ownership (e.g., Ross et al., this volume).

13. *Distributive justice and moral development.* Ownership confers power upon owners in relation to others. Anne may either permit or deny others' access to her book. In controlling access, she may learn to consider others' needs and welfare. She may share or donate her property to others in need, or trade property based on principles of equity (Rochat, this volume). Thus ownership and property provide a rich domain for studying the development of certain moral principles.

14. *Socialization.* To the extent that ownership governs interactions with objects as well as rights and obligations with respect to objects,

children must come to understand and adhere to the relevant principles of entitlement. Ownership provides a specific domain in which parents' socialization can be studied (Ross et al., this volume). Moreover, socializing influences may be bi-directional, as children negotiate and influence the principles adopted in their families. Studies of ownership may help specify the scope and limits of children's influences on the socializing process.

15. Social recognition. Ownership of an object is meaningful to the extent that it is recognized and respected by others. In this sense, ownership is mind-dependent; Kalish and Anderson (this volume) consider two senses, one mild, one stronger, in which ownership can be viewed this way. Because ownership of an object can only be respected to the extent that people know the object is owned, owners must communicate their ownership status to effectively protect their rights. For this reason, owners must infer or ascertain whether others know that certain property belongs to them, and take action to make their ownership apparent (Rose, 1985).

16. Conflicts. Ownership is at the root of many property disputes. It is a common source of conflicts in young children (e.g., Ross, 1996), and an enduring cause of conflict among individual adults, groups, and nations. It could be that ownership disputes simply result from misunderstandings and self-interest. Alternatively, disputes might arise because of properties specific to the cognitive systems underlying reasoning about ownership. If so, ownership disputes may provide valuable hints about how people reason about ownership. Conversely, knowledge concerning ownership may improve understanding of ownership disputes, perhaps including how they can better be avoided and resolved.

17. First- versus third-person perspectives. People prefer things that they own over those they do not. Such preferences arise in judgments of how favorable objects are (mere ownership effect; Beggan, 1992), judgments of how much objects are worth (endowment effect; e.g., Kahneman, Knetsch, & Thaler, 1990), and tests of object memorability (Cunningham, Turk, Macdonald, & Macrae, 2008), and these preferences may also extend to other species (Brosnan, this volume). Such preferences may sometimes be irrational—why should merely owning an object make it seem more valuable? But often greater attentiveness to one's property seems like a natural consequence of ownership. As Wilson and Sperber (2004, p. 610) note, in a very different context, "while we are all likely to notice the sound of glass breaking in our vicinity, we are likely to attend to it more, and process it more deeply, when our memory and inference mechanisms identify it as the sound of our glass breaking."

18. The self and self-image. It has long been claimed that ownership is linked to the self and self-image (e.g., James, 1890). For instance, Belk (1991) argues that many owned things are regarded as extensions of the self, and hence treated as having special properties. Similar views underlie certain accounts of the development of ownership in children; Rochat (this volume; 2010) views children's sense of ownership over objects as arising from infants extending their sense of self (including responsibility for their own actions) to objects (also see Humphrey, 1992, Chapter 18).

19. Psychology and law. An entire branch of law, property law, is concerned with ownership. Ownership is not just important in modern legal systems, but has always been a concern of the law, as evidenced by the preoccupation with ownership in early legal codes, such as the Laws of Manu (1500 BC). Understanding ownership may be informative about the psychological basis of law, the effects of law on psychology, and the degree to which psychological intuitions are consistent with law.

20. Mental illness and crime. Unusual ownership-related behaviors characterize certain mental health conditions, such as compulsive hoarding (Steketee & Frost, 2003; Preston, Muroff, & Wengrovitz, 2009) and kleptomania; the same is true for criminal activities, such as shoplifting, robbery, and vandalism. Increasing our understanding of ownership may influence how we view these varied phenomena. Perhaps some of these occur because of peculiarities in how certain people reason about ownership.

21. A meeting of domains. At the heart of reasoning about ownership seems to be the concept *owns*, which is arguably primitive (Jackendoff, 1992). At the same time, reasoning about ownership plausibly draws on, or connects with, many other diverse types of reasoning. As noted earlier, reasoning about ownership may be tied to moral reasoning, to social obligations, and to the self and self-concept. Certain ownership inferences may also depend on associative learning (Blake & Harris, this volume), counterfactual or causal reasoning (Friedman, 2010), assessments of creativity (Kanngiesser, Gjersoe, & Hood, 2010), and on people's ability to draw the distinction between natural kinds and artifacts (Friedman et al., this volume). It will be an interesting challenge to explain how these diverse forms of reasoning join together to make people's reasoning about ownership possible.

References

Beggan, J. K. (1992). On the social nature of nonsocial perception: The mere ownership effect. *Journal of Personality and Social Psychology*, 62, 229–237.

Belk, R. W. (1991). The ineluctable mysteries of possessions. In F. W. Rudmin (Ed.), *To have possessions: A handbook of ownership and property. Journal of Social Behavior and Personality*, 6, 17–55.

Blackstone, W. (1766). *Commentaries on the laws of England, Book II.* Oxford: Clarendon Press.

Blake, P. R., & Harris, P. L. (2011). Early representations of ownership. In H. Ross & O. Friedman (Eds.), *Origins of ownership of property. New Directions for Child and Adolescent Development*, 132, 39–51.

Brosnan, S. F. (2011). Property in nonhuman primates. In H. Ross & O. Friedman (Eds.), *Origins of ownership of property. New Directions for Child and Adolescent Development, 132*, 9–22.

Brown, D. E. (1991). *Human universals.* New York, NY: McGraw-Hill.

Cunningham, S. J., Turk, D. J., Macdonald, L. M., & Macrae, C. N. (2008). Yours or mine? Ownership and memory. *Consciousness and Cognition, 17*, 312–318.

Fiske, A. P. (1992). The four elementary forms of sociality: Framework for a unified theory of social relations. *Psychological Review, 99*, 689–723.

Friedman, O. (2010). Necessary for possession: How people reason about the acquisition of ownership. *Personality and Social Psychology Bulletin, 36*, 1161–1169.

Friedman, O., Neary, K. R., Defeyter, M. A., & Malcolm, S. L. (2011). Ownership and object history. In H. Ross & O. Friedman (Eds.), *Origins of ownership of property. New Directions for Child and Adolescent Development, 132*, 79–89.

Humphrey, N. (1992). *A history of the mind: Evolution and the birth of consciousness.* New York, NY: Simon & Schuster.

Jackendoff, R. S. (1992). *Languages of the mind.* Cambridge, MA: MIT Press.

James, W. (1890). *The principles of psychology.* New York, NY: Holt.

Kahneman, D., Knetsch, J., & Thaler, R. (1990). Experimental tests of the endowment effect and the Coase theorem. *Journal of Political Economy, 98*, 1325–1348.

Kalish, C. W., & Anderson, C. D. (2011). Ownership as a social status. In H. Ross & O. Friedman (Eds.), *Origins of ownership of property. New Directions for Child and Adolescent Development, 132*, 65–78.

Kanngiesser, P., Gjersoe, N., & Hood, B. M. (2010).Transfer of property ownership following creative labour in preschool children and adults. *Psychological Science, 21*, 1236-1241.

Noles, N. S., & Keil, F. C. (2011). Exploring ownership in a developmental context. In H. Ross & O. Friedman (Eds.), *Origins of ownership of property. New Directions for Child and Adolescent Development, 132*, 91–103.

Olson, K. R., & Shaw, A. (in press). "No fair, Copycat!": What children's response to plagiarism tells us about their understanding of ideas. *Developmental Science.*

Preston, S. D., Muroff, J. R., & Wengrovitz, S. M. (2009). Investigating the mechanisms of hoarding from an experimental perspective. *Depression and Anxiety, 26*, 425–437.

Rochat, P. (2010). The innate sense of the body develops to become a public affair by 2–3 years. *Neuropsychologia, 48*, 738–745.

Rochat, P. (2011). Possession and morality in early development. In H. Ross & O. Friedman (Eds.), *Origins of ownership of property. New Directions for Child and Adolescent Development, 132*, 23–38.

Rose, C. M. (1985). Possession as the origin of property. *University of Chicago Law Review, 52*, 73–88.

Ross, H. S. (1996). Negotiating principles of entitlement in sibling property disputes. *Developmental Psychology, 32*, 90–101.

Ross, H., Conant, C., & Vickar, M. (2011). Property rights and the resolution of social conflict. In H. Ross & O. Friedman (Eds.), *Origins of ownership of property. New Directions for Child and Adolescent Development, 132*, 53–64.

Snare, F. (1972). The concept of property. *American Philosophical Quarterly, 9*, 200–206.

Stake, J. E. (2004). The property 'instinct.' *Philosophical Transactions of the Royal Society B: Biological Sciences, 359*, 1763–1774.

Steketee, G., & Frost, R. O. (2003). Compulsive hoarding: Current status of the research. *Clinical Psychology Review, 23*, 905–927.

Wilson, M., & Daly, M. (1992). The man who mistook his wife for a chattel. In J. H. Barkow, L. Cosmides, & J. Tooby (Eds.), *The adapted mind. Evolutionary psychology and the generation of culture.* New York, NY: Oxford University Press.

Wilson, D., & Sperber, D. (2004). Relevance theory. In L. Horn & G. Ward (Eds.), *The handbook of pragmatics.* Oxford, England: Blackwell.

ORI FRIEDMAN *is associate professor of psychology, University of Waterloo. Waterloo, ON, Canada. E-mail: friedman@uwaterloo.ca.*

HILDY ROSS *is professor emeritus, University of Waterloo. Waterloo, ON, Canada. E-mail: hross@waterloo.ca; webpage: http://familystudies.uwaterloo.ca.*

NEW DIRECTIONS FOR CHILD AND ADOLESCENT DEVELOPMENT • DOI: 10.1002/cd

Brosnan, S. F. (2011). Property in nonhuman primates. In H. Ross & O. Friedman (Eds.), *Origins of ownership of property. New Directions for Child and Adolescent Development, 132,* 9–22.

2

Property in Nonhuman Primates

Sarah F. Brosnan

ABSTRACT

Property is rare in most nonhuman primates, most likely because their lifestyles are not conducive to it. Nonetheless, just because these species do not frequently maintain property does not mean that they lack the propensity to do so. Primates show respect for possession, as well as behaviors related to property, such as irrational decision making regarding property (e.g., the endowment effect) and barter. The limiting factor in species other than humans is likely the lack of social and institutional controls for maintaining property. By comparing primates and humans, we gain a better understanding of how human property concepts have evolved.

I thank Bart Wilson for many conversations that helped to formulate these ideas and the participants in the symposium on ownership at the 6th annual meeting of the Cognitive Development Society (October 15–17, 2009, in San Antonio, TX) for stimulating discussion surrounding these ideas. Funding to the author was provided by a National Science Foundation Human and Social Dynamics Grant (SES 0729244) and an NSF CAREER Award (SES 0847351).

Property is a concept taken almost for granted among modern Western peoples (at least, until there is a dispute over it). We not only have an intuitive understanding of mine and yours, but also a series of social norms, rules, and governance structures set up to manage the relationships dictated by the presence of property. Yet for all of our focus on property, little is known about how this concept evolved. How did we become the only species on earth to have these complex rules of ownership and succession? It is possible that our sense of property is emergent in humans, a result of our cognitive complexity or advanced culture (e.g., Kalish & Anderson, this volume; Noles & Keil, this volume). On the other hand, it is also possible that these complexities are continuations of the basic property or possession behaviors seen in some other species.

In fact, there are other species that seem to have at least elements of a sense of property (Stake, 2004). Among primates, there is evidence for a sense of property both from observations and from experimental situations. Notably, several primate species behave as though objects in the possession of others belong to that individual (Kummer & Cords, 1990; Sigg & Falett, 1985). Moreover caching species, such as scrub jays and kangaroo rats, hide food items for later retrieval, and may even move them around to avoid snooping competitors (Dally, Emery, & Clayton, 2006; Emery & Clayton, 2001; Preston & Jacobs, 2005). Many of these caching species are phylogenetically quite distantly related to humans, indicating that this behavior emerged in several species based on similar ecological constraints, known in evolutionary terms as convergence,[1] and may be widespread through the animal kingdom.

To understand the emergence of our sense of property, it is useful to explore the behavior both broadly within the animal kingdom and more specifically among other primate species, particularly the apes, as they are

---

[1]Convergence is an evolutionary mechanism in which different species evolve similar characteristics (here, property-related behaviors) because of similar environmental constraints. The other mechanism I discuss is homology, in which different species share similar characteristics because both are descended from a common ancestor who displayed the behavior. As a simple example, both blue jays and eagles share wings through homology because the mutual common ancestor to both species also had wings. On the other hand, blue jays, bats, and butterflies all have wings through convergence; their mutual common ancestor did not have wings. Instead, the benefits of taking advantage of an open ecological niche, the air, provided pressure that increased the likelihood of wings developing as the appropriate mutations arose. Note that a close phylogenetic relationship may imply a homologous relationship, but does not guarantee it; the traits could also have arisen independently through convergent processes. Although the distinction is critical and often overlooked, for the purposes of this chapter it is largely irrelevant whether a particular shared trait evolved through homologous or convergent processes because we are interested in the presence or absence of property-related behaviors in other species and are not developing a phylogenetic tree based on this data to trace the evolution of these behaviors.

NEW DIRECTIONS FOR CHILD AND ADOLESCENT DEVELOPMENT • DOI: 10.1002/cd

our closest phylogenetic kin. Studying how property in these species is different from (or similar to) that of other species, especially in concert with an understanding of the environmental characteristics that may have led to convergences, can help clarify how the human property concept evolved.

Defining Property

Among humans, the law is the institution perhaps most interested in property, and so is a good starting point. The law defines property with respect to the relationship between people that gives rise to the agreement that one object is mine and another is yours (Bentham, 1914). Bentham went so far as to assert that property did not exist before the laws regulating it. However, this definition conflicts with the folk notion of property as a relationship between an object and a person, and denies out of hand the possibility that property could be based on behaviors or concepts present in other species (Stake, 2004).

There is evidence in favor of this latter position. Children as young as eighteen to twenty-four months of age show inferences about the ownership of property (Fasig, 2000). Such inferences may be due to mechanisms such as following the heuristic that the first possessor of an object is the owner (Friedman & Neary, 2007; Friedman, Neary, Defeyter, & Malcolm, this volume). Although even at this early age ideas about ownership could be learned through interactions with adults of the species, this early start indicates the possibility of a predisposition towards property. Moreover, other species seem to have some basic behaviors that are consistent with the idea that a thing can belong to a specific individual. For instance, some species show begging and sharing behavior in relation to food, instead of simply taking by force the food that is desired (e.g., chimpanzees; Goodall, 1986), which indicates that food is seen as having an owner. Several species of nonhuman primates behave as if possession is a special state. In these primates, individuals do not attempt to take objects that are in another's possession, even if the possessor is the subordinate individual (Kummer, 1991; Kummer & Cords, 1990). Interestingly, the U.S. legal system also prioritizes possession when dealing with property disputes (Stake, 2004). This phenomenon, termed "respect for possession," will be discussed in more detail later but provides strong evidence for a basic sense of property shared between humans and other species.

Thus, it seems reasonable to assume that possession of property is not an emergent property of human institutions, in particular the legal system, and that some precursors to the behaviors and attitudes that led to property as seen in the human sense can be seen in other species. Looking for these precursor behaviors in other species can help to identify the ways in which property evolved and pin down criteria that may be important for

NEW DIRECTIONS FOR CHILD AND ADOLESCENT DEVELOPMENT • DOI: 10.1002/cd

the development of the concept of property. To begin, we first need an operational definition of what is meant by property and which specific behaviors would be evidence for its presence.

To maintain property, an individual needs to maintain control over an object that is not a part of its body. Of course, property can be lost, stolen, or transferred, so permanent maintenance of access is not a necessary requirement for property. From a biological perspective, there are two different forms of property: that which is physically in one's possession and that which is maintained despite being outside of one's physical control. For the sake of simplicity, I refer to these, respectively, as possession and ownership.

Maintaining possession is likely the simplest form of property. In this case, an individual maintains an item by keeping that item under its physical control at all times. Functionally, this is defined as the individual touching the item in some way (in an appendage, mouth, beak, etc.). Although in the most trivial sense, this form of property is essentially ubiquitous, as any time an individual picks up a piece of food to consume, it is in its possession, possession also extends beyond this. Individuals may maintain possession for more extended periods of time, in which case norms or standards of conduct for how items in another's possession should be treated may be formed. For instance, among ravens, individuals that possess an item can expect to maintain it, even if a larger or otherwise more dominant individual approaches. These norms are upheld through third-party interactions in which uninvolved third parties will attack those that steal from another raven (Heinrich, 1999). Such norms indicate that possession has a special status in these species.

The second form of property, ownership, is that over which one maintains control even when the item is not in one's possession. This may include such resources as dens, nests, or home ranges, although these are typically group resources that are defended by and shared by all the members of the social group. In a few species, ownership includes another critical resource, food. In species, such as squirrels, that cache food items, individuals maintain property without possession, and reclaim those objects when they need them for survival, such as in the scrub jays discussed earlier. Note that such property need not be due to respect for ownership; in many cases property may remain under the individual's control either because it is hidden from others, or because the individual that has ownership or possession is dominant, so others cannot easily take the items.

What seems to set human property apart from that of other species is the extensive reliance on the goodwill of others to assist in the maintenance of ownership (e.g., property outside of one's possession) through third-party reinforcement. In humans, this takes the form of both institutional structures to maintain ownership rights (police force, legal system) and the tendency of humans to respect each other's property ownership. As mentioned previously with respect to the ravens, third-party norms do exist in other species, but typically only for current possessions, and not with respect to ownership. This may be due to the inability of other species to convey information beyond the immediate, as can be done with language. This means that third-party interventions can only occur in situations in which the transgression was witnessed by a potential supporter (Brosnan, Grady, Lambeth, Schapiro, & Beran, 2008). Moreover, although many of us may resort to the legal system to reclaim property that has been taken from us, the truth is that in a well-functioning society, this recourse is required surprisingly rarely, particularly with respect to how often property we own is left outside of our immediate possession. People routinely leave their jackets on a seat during the intermission at a play or their grill on the deck of their house or apartment and seem to expect that these items will still be there upon their return. And in fact, they usually are. The question, then, is what is it that makes human property so different?

Property in Primates

Property in primates is rare, and exists almost exclusively in the form of possession, not ownership. Primates do maintain territories, or home ranges, sometimes individually and sometimes in groups. These can be considered a form of property, although given the frequency of territorial behavior across the animal kingdom, this tells us very little about the evolution of property. Unlike some other animals, no primate (outside of some humans) relies on caching as a major food source. This is most likely an ecological constraint. Food is the most obvious object for animals to store as property, as it is essential for survival. However, primates typically live in areas where at least some food source is available year-round, allowing them to forage for food as they need it. Moreover, caching is impractical for most primates; they typically eat foods that do not store well, such as fruit, negating the utility of maintaining food for any extended period before consuming it. Thus, the opportunities for food as property, particularly in the form of ownership, are limited.

Primates behave in other ways that are indicative of some concept of possession. One primary manifestation is the remarkable respect for the rights of the possessor of an object shown by some species (Kummer, 1991; Kummer & Cords, 1990). Chimpanzees show a "respect for possession" that allows individuals to maintain possession of an item, even in the presence of the alpha male (Goodall, 1972). This ability is not limited to the apes, either. Several monkey species show evidence of respect of food possession (Perry, 1997; Sigg & Falett, 1985). Outside of the realm of food, hamadryas baboon males show respect for the females in each other's harems (Kummer, Götz, & Angst, 1974), not attempting to mate with them or claim them even though these harem units interact with each other on a daily basis.

What qualifies as "possession" varies between species. In some species, even holding an object is not sufficient; individuals must be able to transport the object for others to respect possession. In an experimental study, long-tailed macaques respected ownership when the owner had possession and was able to carry the object. Respect for possession broke down, though, even when the owner had possession of the object, in two cases. First was if the possessor could not carry it with them because it was tethered to the floor. Second was if the object had a trailing string (similar to a kite tail) that extended beyond the possessor's immediate vicinity. In either case, the more dominant individual typically took control of the object. In these macaques, proximity was also not sufficient to maintain possession (Kummer & Cords, 1990).

Not all species have such stringent requirements for possession. Among hamadryas baboons, proximity is sufficient to trigger respect for possession, and in some cases even the memory of a previous possession may be sufficient to trigger this response (Sigg & Falett, 1985; see also, Friedman et al., this volume). This variation in experimental outcomes is most likely due to differences in the socio-ecology of the different species. Hamadryas baboons evolved in a situation in which a valuable possession (e.g., harem females) was in proximity, but not under physical control, widening the concept of possession in this species.

One of the challenges in assessing possession is that it is difficult to determine whether possession is respected as a norm versus for more prosaic self-serving reasons. In many cases, it appears that non-norm-based accounts exist to explain animals' interactions over possessions. For instance, food calls may serve to identify possession, which could indicate a norm. On the other hand, the food call may also indicate how likely a challenge is from the possessor. Thus, failure to obtain the food after hearing a food call may be due to nonpossessors avoiding a potential fight rather than respect for possession (Gros-Luis, 2004; Krebs, 1982). Similarly, among chimpanzees it has been hypothesized that the intense motivation to keep a food reward is what allows lower-ranking individuals to sometimes maintain possession of a carcass following a monkey hunt, rather than a social norm respecting possession (Goodall, 1986). Finally, it is also likely that "possession norms" are due at least in part to reciprocity. High-ranking individuals may refrain from taking the property of those that rank below them to keep those lower-ranking individuals as grooming or mating partners (de Waal, 2005).

These different mechanisms make assessing "pure" respect for possession difficult. Humans, too, may fail to take resources for many of these same reasons. However, there are some situations in which the evidence does indicate the presence of social norms related to possession. In some species, third-party interventions may reduce the frequency with which owners are challenged for their possessions. Although in these cases the nonpossessor may not attack for self-serving reasons, the fact that a third party intervenes indicates the presence of possession-related norms. Among long-tailed macaques, possession was more likely to be challenged for older possessors, who are less likely to scream and, hence, attract support, which the authors propose as evidence of third-party norms supporting possession rights (Kummer & Cords, 1990).

However, none of these studies gets at ownership, or possessions outside of one's immediate control. This is partly due to the lack of situations in which ownership appears in the wild. Thus an alternative approach, which allows for more explicit control, is to investigate these phenomena in the laboratory. In fact, chimpanzees do seem to recognize that they "own" something beyond their immediate possession in the laboratory. Although in laboratory studies subjects are typically given a food reward for each desired response, chimpanzees are willing to work for rewards (food items or tokens) that collect in a specified location and then are given to the subjects en masse (Cowles, 1937; Sousa & Matsuzawa, 2001; Wolfe, 1936). This indicates that, at least on some level, the chimpanzees understand that the rewards are "theirs," even though they are not in their possession. Chimpanzees understand this even if there are several collections of tokens or food, only one of which contains items that are "theirs."

As part of another study, chimpanzees were tested in pairs in which each individual could trade tokens for food rewards. These tokens consisted of symbols that represented various foods which were made available in the study; these symbols had been used by each of the chimpanzees since infancy and so had strong associations. The chimpanzees each had a separate food bin, with different food items available to them than were available to their partners. Each could obtain only the foods that were present in their bin by trading the appropriate token for it, despite being able to see their partner's available foods. Moreover, all tokens for foods available for either chimpanzee were available at all times, so chimpanzees had access to tokens that did not match their available food rewards. The only cost to these incorrect trades was time; the chimpanzees were allowed an unlimited number of exchanges to acquire their foods. Despite this, the chimpanzees learned very rapidly that they could acquire the foods only from their own bin, and did not request the foods from their partners' bins (Brosnan & Beran, 2009). This indicates that they understood at least on some level that those foods were not "theirs," as determined by the experimenter.

Even so, this still does not fully get at ownership, as the human experimenter acted as a mediator. One difficulty with testing property in chimpanzees is that though food items represent the strongest level of motivation, because of this they are also unlikely to hold them for a long period without eating them. Thus, it is difficult to use food items as part of a study involving property. However, with a little creativity, certain aspects of property may be tested using paradigms that get around the problems inherent in food. For instance, tokens can be used that represent foods (and can later be traded for foods, as in the study discussed) or food that cannot be consumed immediately can be used. Both of these approaches have been used successfully, as is discussed later on.

The Endowment Effect. The issue of property can be addressed tangentially, by testing for characteristics of property known to be exhibited by humans. One common finding is that humans tend to behave irrationally when making decisions about their property. One way in which this manifests is in a phenomenon referred to as the endowment effect, in which individuals will pay more to keep an item that is in their possession than they would have previously paid to obtain the same item. This implies that individuals value what is in their possession simply because of that fact, even when there has not been enough time to develop a sentimental attachment to it or additional uses for it (Jones & Brosnan, 2008; Kahneman, Knetsch, & Thaler, 1990).

Chimpanzees, too, increase their preference for items in their possession above and beyond the value they indicated when the object was not in their possession (Brosnan, Jones et al., 2007). In this study, chimpanzees were given a series of sessions to determine how preferences changed dependent upon possession. One session served to verify their preferences; additional sessions offered them opportunities to exchange what they were given initially for something else. There was no cost to trading other than the few seconds the trade took. To make sure that the chimpanzees were sufficiently motivated, foods were used instead of tokens representing foods. The chosen foods were difficult to consume rapidly; one item was peanut butter that had to be removed from a PVC tube and the other was a frozen juice stick that subjects preferred not to bite into.

To establish preferences, chimpanzees were asked to choose between the two foods. To determine whether the chimpanzees preferred to maintain possession of those items that they had in their possession, chimpanzees were given each of the items individually (in separate sessions) and then immediately offered the opportunity to exchange for the other.[2] As with humans, as a group chimpanzees were more likely to hold onto whichever food item they were given than was expected, based on their preference for the items in the choice session. Individually, almost half of the chimpanzees followed this pattern, choosing to hold onto whichever item they had been given. All chimpanzees were willing to exchange food items away when something of greater value (a banana) was offered, so their disinclination to exchange cannot be explained by concern about the risks inherent in trading away food or the reliability of the human experimenter.

Interestingly, this holds for foods, but not for nonfood objects with which they interact. When the same study was repeated using two familiar toys, the chimpanzees actually preferred to exchange, perhaps valuing the interaction with the experimenter over the possibilities of the

---

[2]In the experiment itself, the order of presentation of these three sessions was randomized among the 36 subjects to ensure that there was no ordering effect influencing responses.

NEW DIRECTIONS FOR CHILD AND ADOLESCENT DEVELOPMENT • DOI: 10.1002/cd

toys themselves (Brosnan, Jones et al., 2007). This indicates that the endowment effect may hold only for those objects that have great utility to the chimpanzees, such as food, and indicates that even within a concept as basic as property, the context of the interaction matters.

More recently, similar studies have been done with orangutans and capuchin monkeys, indicating that they, too, show an endowment effect (Flemming, Jones, Stoinski, Mayo, & Brosnan, in review; Lakshminarayanan, Chen, & Santos, 2008). Capuchin monkeys also exhibit loss aversion, showing a preference for outcomes framed as a reward over those framed as a loss despite the actual distribution of outcomes being equal (Chen, Lakshminarayanan, & Santos, 2006). This is another "irrational" behavior that is often linked with the endowment effect. Taken with the results on chimpanzees, it appears that this suite of irrational behaviors occurs in primates in general, supporting the idea that concepts of property are broadly distributed in the primates, and likely throughout the animal kingdom.

Barter. Another element of property is that it can be used to obtain more or different property through trade and barter. In barter, an individual can trade an object in their possession or under their ownership for another object possessed or owned by someone else. In fact, this, in concert with specialization, is one of the core tenets of economic theory. As such, there has been quite a bit of interest in whether other species can barter. Adam Smith famously quoted that "It [barter, to exchange one thing for another] is common to all men, and to be found in no other race of animals, which seem to know neither this nor any other species of contracts… Nobody ever saw a dog make a fair and deliberate exchange of one bone for another with another dog" (Smith, 1776). Barter has not been reported in wild populations; however, chimpanzees and other species do share food (e.g., Feistner & McGrew, 1989; Hockings et al., 2007), which is a related behavior. There are also a few captive observations of spontaneous behavior, which may indicate the presence of exchange behavior in primates (Paquette, 1992).

Most studies thus far have required subjects to trade a token to a human experimenter for another food item, which both chimpanzees and capuchin monkeys do easily (Brosnan & de Waal, 2004, 2005; Hyatt & Hopkins, 1998). In fact, both of these species also seem to understand the tokens as symbols, and can work with them flexibly (Addessi, Crescimbene, & Visalberghi, 2007; Addessi, Mancini, Crescimbene, Padoa-Schioppa, & Visalberghi, 2008; Savage-Rumbaugh, Rumbaugh, & Boysen, 1978). However, this only indicates that primates can learn associations, but does not require the subject to actually give up something of value to obtain something else. It is this latter, more costly, exchange behavior that we typically consider when discussing barter.

Several studies on barter of food items have found that chimpanzees are not only able to do this, but also are very intelligent in how they barter with humans (Lefebvre, 1982; Lefebvre & Hewitt, 1986). In these studies, chimpanzees were rational, trading foods they did not like for those that they did, and trading more readily when the difference in value between the food items was greater. They were also intelligent; the experimenter would take any size food item in exchange for another, and the chimpanzees learned to return very small bits of food, or even just a daub of saliva. This behavior maximized their intake of both foods. A recent study replicated these findings with a larger adult sample of chimpanzees (Brosnan, Grady et al., 2008). In this study, chimpanzees received an endowment of 30 food items (of varying types) and were given the opportunity to exchange those items for other food items. Again, chimpanzees never traded food items for those that were less preferred, and they always traded disfavored foods for much more preferred items. When food items were close in value, subjects typically did not exchange. This behavior, similar to that seen in the endowment effect study discussed earlier, indicates that chimpanzees are hesitant to give up an item in their possession, possibly because of the risks of trade.

Note that all of the studies on barter discussed have one significant confound—they all involve trading with humans, rather than a subject of the same species. This makes it difficult to extrapolate their behavior to natural circumstances due to the difference in the type of relationship between primate conspecifics (e.g., members of the same species) and primates and humans. In the latter, the humans occupy an atypical, omniscient/omnipotent role, which may make the monkeys and apes react differently than they would to a conspecific. However, human/primate barter is the norm because of the difficulty inherent in getting primates to give up a food reward to another individual. Even a well-trained chimpanzee is unlikely to voluntarily trade away a preferred food item in their possession for another. This can be avoided through the use of symbolic tokens, rather than foods.

In a recent study, chimpanzees were given tokens that bore symbols representing foods, rather than the food items themselves (Brosnan & Beran, 2009; also see previous). These chimpanzees had trained to use these symbols as infants, and each subject had at least 20 years' experience with them, so they easily understood the token/food associations (controls were run to verify that this was the case). In a series of studies, chimpanzees were given several tokens. Some of these could be exchanged with the experimenter to obtain foods; others were worthless to them, but could be used by another chimpanzee (their partner). Although chimpanzees initially were hesitant to do so, they ultimately learned to trade tokens among themselves prior to exchanging tokens for foods with the experimenter, which maximized the number of foods each chimpanzee could receive. During this time there was experimenter oversight of the interactions; the experimenter would not exchange with either ape until each chimpanzee had traded a token of their choice with their partner (they could simply return the token their partner had given to them). Once experimenter oversight was removed, however, all trade behavior ceased within the first session. Instead, the chimpanzees simply returned all of their tokens to the experimenter, and received many fewer food items than were available.

This test indicates two interesting findings. First, chimpanzees are capable of cognitively understanding trade, and will do so in a way that benefits themselves and their partner. Second, experimenter control is apparently necessary for successful barter among captive adult chimpanzees. These together indicate that there is significant risk inherent in trading among chimpanzees. This may be due to the lack of recourse if the partner fails to complete the trade. Humans have solved this problem through the introduction of legal and policing systems that can enforce appropriate trade behavior on others, minimizing the risk of any given interaction. Chimpanzees, lacking the ability to communicate beyond the immediate (e.g., narrative language), would have difficulty with third-party reinforcement except in situations in which the third party witnessed the interaction (Brosnan, Grady et al., 2008). Thus, it is likely that, despite an apparent lack of cognitive limitations, trading behavior has not evolved due to the high costs inherent in a trading system without oversight and recourse. It is possible that other species that have less competitive social interactions may show more of a tendency towards barter behavior, but it is likely that the lack of narrative language limits the development of extensive barter in all species except humans.

Conclusion

Taken as a whole, the evidence supports the idea that, counter to Bentham's (1914) assertion, there are biological bases for property. Although no other species has developed a system of property ownership so complex and far-reaching as humans have, nonhuman primates appear to have expectations related to objects, or social norms, that are in their or another's possession. This possession-centered concept of property makes evolutionary sense; not only is it easier to defend property that is in one's possession, but the legal enforcements required for ownership are difficult or impossible to enforce without the development of language.

Norms regarding possession are not the only property-related feature shared between humans and other species. Experimental studies in nonhuman primates have found evidence of behaviors (such as barter) and psychological features (such as the endowment effect) that are seen in human property-related behavior. Perhaps the critical difference between humans and other species is that in other species, individuals may assume that they will need to enforce their right to their property by themselves, without any recourse, whereas humans can rely on others to assist in maintaining property rights. Even if other species have the necessary cognitive underpinnings, such as third-party enforcement of norms or well-developed reciprocity, they still lack the ability to communicate about other individuals' misdeeds. This limits their ability either to request assistance in reclaiming property or to warn others about those that do not respect property, which seriously limits the extent to which these norms may develop.

Thus, the critical development for humans may have been the emergence of two features; first, a norm that indicates that property *outside* of one's immediate possession or control is still property, and should not be taken by others (e.g., ownership; see also Rochat, this volume), and second, the language skills necessary to recruit the support of others in the maintenance of this norm. Together these could have led to the development of formalized legal systems that protect ownership of property even when it is outside of one's immediate control or when an instance of theft takes place beyond the observation of others. Although human property concepts differ from those of other species, this comparative approach sheds light on the biological basis of the emergence of property in humans and other animals.

References

Addessi, E., Crescimbene, L., & Visalberghi, E. (2007). Do capuchin monkeys (*Cebus apella*) use tokens as symbols? *Proceedings of the Royal Society of London B, 274,* 2709–2715.

Addessi, E., Mancini, A., Crescimbene, L., Padoa-Schioppa, C., & Visalberghi, E. (2008). Preference transitivity and symbolic representation in capuchin monkeys (*Cebus apella*). *PLoS ONE, 3*(6), e2414.

Bentham, J. (1914). Of property. In E. Dumont (Ed.), *The theory of legislation, Vol 1. Principles of civil code, Part I.* Oxford, England: Oxford University Press.

Brosnan, S. F., & Beran, M. J. (2009). Bartering behavior between conspecifics in chimpanzees, *Pan troglodytes. Journal of Comparative Psychology, 123,* 181–194.

Brosnan, S. F., & de Waal, F. B. M. (2004). A concept of value during experimental exchange in brown capuchin monkeys. *Folia primatologica, 75,* 317–330.

Brosnan, S. F., & de Waal, F. B. M. (2005). Responses to a simple barter task in chimpanzees, *Pan troglodytes. Primates, 46,* 173–182.

Brosnan, S. F., Grady, M., Lambeth, S., Schapiro, S., & Beran, M. J. (2008). Chimpanzee autarky. *PLoS ONE, 3*(1), e1518.

Brosnan, S. F., Jones, O. D., Mareno, M. C., Richardson, A. S., Lambeth, S. P., & Schapiro, S. J. (2007). Endowment effects in chimpanzees. *Current Biology, 17,* 1704–1707.

Chen, M. K., Lakshminarayanan, V., & Santos, L. R. (2006). How basic are behavioral biases? Evidence from capuchin monkey trading behavior. *Journal of Political Economy, 114*(3), 517–537.

Cowles, J. T. (1937). Food-tokens as incentives for learning by chimpanzees. *Comparative Psychology Monographs, 14,* 1–96.

Dally, J. M., Emery, N. J., & Clayton, N. S. (2006). Food-caching western scrub-jays keep track of who was watching when. *Science, 312,* 1662–1665.

de Waal, F. B. M. (2005). *Our inner ape: A leading primatologist explains why we are who we are.* New York, NY: Riverhead.

Emery, N. J., & Clayton, N. S. (2001). Effects of experience and social context on pro-spective caching strategies by scrub jays. *Nature, 414,* 443–446.

Fasig, L. G. (2000). Toddlers' understanding of ownership: Implications for self-concept development. *Social Development, 9*(3), 370–382.

Feistner, A. T. C., & McGrew, W. C. (1989). Food-sharing in primates: A critical review. In P. K. Seth & S. Seth (Eds.), *Perspectives in Primate Biology.* New Delhi: Today & Tomorrow's Printers and Publishers.

Flemming, T. E., Jones, O. D., Stoinski, T. S., Mayo, L., & Brosnan, S. F. (in review). The endowment effect in orangutans. Manuscript submitted for publication.

Friedman, O., & Neary, K. R. (2007). Determining who owns what: Do children infer ownership from first possession? *Cognition, 107,* 829–849.

Friedman, O., Neary, K. R., Defeyter, M. A., & Malcolm, S. L. (2011). Ownership and object history. In H. Ross & O. Friedman (Eds.), *Origins of ownership of property. New Directions for Child and Adolescent Development, 132,* 79–89.

Goodall, J. (1972). *In the Shadow of Man.* Boston, MA: Houghton Mifflin Company.

Goodall, J. (1986). *The Chimpanzees of Gombe.* Cambridge, MA: The Belknap Press of Harvard University Press.

Gros-Luis, J. (2004). The function of food-associated calls in white-faced capuchin monkeys, *Cebus capucinus,* from the perspective of the signaller. *Animal Behavior, 67,* 431-440.

Heinrich, B. (1999). *Mind of the Raven.* New York, NY: HarperCollins.

Hockings, K. J., Humle, T., Anderson, J. R., Biro, D., Sousa, C., Ohashi, G., & Matsuzawa, T. (2007). Chimpanzees share forbidden fruit. *PLoS ONE* 2 (9), e886.

Hyatt, C. W., & Hopkins, W. D. (1998). Interspecies object exchange: Bartering in apes? *Behavioural Processes, 42,* 177–187.

Jones, O. D., & Brosnan, S. F. (2008). An evolutionary perspective on the endowment effect. *William and Mary Law Review, 49,* 1935–1990.

Kahneman, D., Knetsch, J. L., & Thaler, R. (1990). Experimental tests of the endowment effect and the Coase theorem. *Journal of Economic Perspectives, 98,* 1325–1348.

Kalish, C. W., & Anderson, C. D. (2011). Ownership as a social status. In H. Ross & O. Friedman (Eds.), *Origins of ownership of property. New Directions for Child and Adolescent Development, 132,* 65–78.

Krebs, J. R. (1982). Territorial defence in the great tit (*Parus major*): Do residents always win? *Behavioral Ecology and Sociobiology, 11,* 185–194.

Kummer, H. (1991). Evolutionary transformations of possessive behavior [Special issue]. *Journal of Social Behavior and Personality, 6*(6), 75–83.

Kummer, H., & Cords, M. (1990). Cues of ownership in long-tailed macaques, *Macaca fascicularis. Animal Behavior, 42,* 529–549.

Kummer, H., Götz, W., & Angst, W. (1974). Triadic differentiation: An inhibitory pro-cess protecting pair bonds in baboons. *Behaviour, 49,* 62–87.

Lakshminarayanan, V., Chen, M. K., & Santos, L. R. (2008). Endowment effect in capuchin monkeys. *Philosophical Transactions of the Royal Society B, 363*(1511), 3837–3844.

Lefebvre, L. (1982). Food exchange strategies in an infant chimpanzee. *Journal of Human Evolution, 11,* 195–204.

Lefebvre, L., & Hewitt, T. A. (1986). Food exchange in captive chimpanzees. In D. M. Taub & F. A. King (Eds.), *Current perspectives in primate social dynamics.* New York, NY: Van Nostrand Reinhold.

Noles, N. S., & Keil, F. C. (2011). Exploring ownership in a developmental context. In H. Ross & O. Friedman (Eds.), *Origins of ownership of property. New Directions for Child and Adolescent Development, 132,* 91–103.

Paquette, D. (1992). Object exchange between captive chimpanzees: A case report. *Human Evolution, 7*(3), 11–15.

Perry, S. (1997). Male-female social relationships in wild white-faced capuchin monkeys, *Cebus capucinus*. *Behaviour, 134*, 477–510.

Preston, S. D., & Jacobs, L. F. (2005). Cache decision making: The effects of competition on cache decisions in Merriam's kangaroo rat (*Dipodomys merriami*). *Journal of Comparative Psychology, 119*(2), 187–196.

Rochat, P. (2011). Possession and morality in early development. In H. Ross & O. Friedman (Eds.), *Origins of ownership of property. New Directions for Child and Adolescent Development, 132*, 23–38.

Savage-Rumbaugh, E. S., Rumbaugh, D. M., & Boysen, S. (1978). Linguistically mediated tool use and exchange by chimpanzees (*Pan troglodytes*). *The Behavioral and Brain Sciences, 4*, 539–554.

Sigg, H., & Falett, J. (1985). Experiments on the respect of possession and property in hamadryas baboons (*Papio hamadryas*). *Animal Behavior, 33*, 978–984.

Smith, A. (1776). *The wealth of nations*. London, England: Adam Smith Institute, The Free Market Think Tank. Retrieved from http://www.adamsmith.org/smith/won /won-b1-c2.html

Sousa, C., & Matsuzawa, T. (2001). The use of tokens as rewards and tools by chimpanzees (*Pan troglodytes*). *Animal Cognition, 4*, 213–221.

Stake, J. E. (2004). The property "instinct". In S. Zeki & O. R. Goodenough (Eds.), *Law and the Brain*, pp. 185–206. Oxford, England: Oxford University Press.

Wolfe, J. B. (1936). Effectiveness of token-rewards for chimpanzees. *Comparative Psychology Monographs, 12*, 1–72.

SARAH F. BROSNAN is assistant professor of psychology & neuroscience at Georgia State University, Atlanta. E-mail: sbrosnan@gsu.edu; webpage: http:// www2.gsu.edu/cebuslab.

NEW DIRECTIONS FOR CHILD AND ADOLESCENT DEVELOPMENT • DOI: 10.1002/cd

Rochat, P. (2011). Possession and morality in early development. In H. Ross & O. Friedman
(Eds.), *Origins of ownership of property. New Directions for Child and Adolescent Development, 132*, 23–38.

3

Possession and Morality in Early Development

Philippe Rochat

Abstract

*From the moment children say "mine!" by two years of age, objects of posses-
sion change progressively from being experienced as primarily unalienable
property (i.e., something that is absolute or nonnegotiable), to being alienable
(i.e., something that is negotiable in reciprocal exchanges). As possession
begins to be experienced as alienable, the child enters "moral space," a socially
normative and evaluative space made of perceived values that are either good
or less good, and where accountability and reputation begin to play a prominent role. The aim of this chapter is to show the close developmental link
between possession and morality.*

Most of the ideas and research presented in this article were developed while
supported by a John Simon Guggenheim Fellowship.

NEW DIRECTIONS FOR CHILD AND ADOLESCENT DEVELOPMENT, no. 132, Summer 2011 © Wiley Periodicals, Inc.
Published online in Wiley Online Library (wileyonlinelibrary.com). • DOI: 10.1002/cd.294

23

The development of a moral sense in children finds a particularly rich soil in the early inclination to possess and appropriate things to the self. The reason is that possession, more often than not, leads to conflicts that need to be resolved to sustain social life.

The goal here is to outline the way young children from various cultural backgrounds develop a sense of ownership and entitlement over objects and people, and how such development correlates with and possibly causes the emergence of a moral sense.

Conflicts over possession and entitlement are pervasive in the whole animal kingdom, from mockingbirds to hermit crabs, and obviously to any mammalian species. We are constantly fighting over territory, sexual partners, food, or any other resources that are scarce and have to be shared. What is arguably different in humans, however, is that such conflicts tend, most of the time, not to be resolved just on the basis of the "lion's share" principle—the coercion of the strongest and the fittest. This is not to say that transcending of the lion's share principle is unique to humans. Other animals show signs of it (see Brosnan, this volume; de Waal, 1996), but such transcending is particularly pronounced and explicitly promoted in all human cultures.

Human cultures evolved common principles and laws (institutions) that try to harness the raw dynamic of the jungle's law. The major function of human cultures is to regulate possession according to explicit principles that enforce the distribution of resources beyond the raw coercive force of natural selection.

All human cultures prescribe what are the rights and privileges of ownership (who "ought" to own what). Such regulation is transmitted and modified from generation to generation, and children have to harness their own proclivity to possess by learning the rules and practices of the cultures in which they grow (see Noles & Keil, this volume).

Brief Outline

First, I will argue that there is an innate propensity to possess in children. What is proposed is that this propensity is probably the major mechanism by which children develop a moral sense, eventually the normative sense of what is right and what is wrong within their parental culture.

In support of this argument, I outline developmental changes in the psychology of possession that emerge between birth and five years of age. Six levels of possession are distinguished, unfolding from birth on. I will show that possession develops from being unalienable (i.e., absolute or nonnegotiable), to being alienable (i.e., tradable and negotiable in exchanges). A crucial point in this model is that when children begin to experience possession as alienable, they are forced to enter "moral space," a socially *evaluative* space made of values that are either good or less good,

NEW DIRECTIONS FOR CHILD AND ADOLESCENT DEVELOPMENT • DOI: 10.1002/cd

and where accountability and reputation begin to play a prominent role (Rochat, 2009; Taylor, 1989).

From this point on, children have to situate themselves in a new, normative space (moral space), and begin to take an *ethical stance* toward others, as well as toward the self in relation to others. This transition marks a change in children's appreciation of others' relations to objects. I provide examples of such progressive ethical effort in three- to five-year-olds growing up in highly contrasted cultural and socioeconomic environments around the world.

In all, the goal is to show that the conceptual notion of property and the moral sense deriving from it participates in the emergence of coconsciousness in children from approximately two to three years of age. Coconsciousness is the inclination to perceive oneself and the surrounding world *through the eyes of others* (Rochat, 2009).

Introduction: Possession and Moral Sense

Social life revolves around the sharing of resources that are typically scarce or "in demand." More often than not supplies are limited. This is the basic economic premise of social life, as first pointed out by Adam Smith (1776/1977). For social life to be sustainable, individuals in a group are required to have some common understanding, or at least a shared "sensibility" as to who possesses what, why some possess more than others, and in general, where possession begins and where it ends. Some closure among social participants on the issue of possession and property is thus a necessary prerequisite of any social life, the cornerstone of what can be said to warrant group cohesion and ultimately survival of the group. It also forms the root of a moral sense.

For most social animals, it appears that possession originates primarily from coercion and the tacit recognition of the lion share principle (the strongest, fittest, and most assertive has precedence in possessing over others). In contradistinction, monkeys and great apes in particular are reported to transcend the natural pervasiveness of the lion share principle (de Waal, 1996). Some individuals of these species are shown to share food, barter grooming for protection, seek alliance via reconciliation, or engage in cooperative acts while hunting and foraging by pairs or in groups.

The meaning of such observations, particularly their interpretation and whether they demonstrate some principled social reasoning and basic moral sense, remains disputed (Silk et al., 2005). In contrast, one would be hard pressed to contest that humans are unmatched in their evolution of systems that formally determine who possesses what and why, and more importantly, who *deserves it and who should have it*. As diverse as human cultures are, all have in common institutions that formally sanction possession, from oral myths and etiquette to honor codes and courts of law.

These cultural institutions are a "sedimentation" of practices that evolved over generations providing guidance and shared collective principles in the just distribution of resources. They dictate some sense of what is right and what is wrong in possessing and sharing available resources, which is not motivated by fear, avoidance, or sheer dominance. They provide norms for agreements to be reached in the just distribution of property among group members.

A good measure of the need for the basic cultural sanction of possession is the fact that six of the Ten Commandments in the Old Testament pertain to the issue of possession and property: *Thou shalt not covet, not steal, not kill, not commit adultery, not bear false witness, have other gods.* All six have something to do with protecting what should be one's own: life, wife, body, and truth. The question of what determines possession is an issue that is at the core of social life.

From antiquity onward, all great Western philosophers grappled with the issue of possession and property. It is also at the center of Eastern philosophies (i.e., all forms of Buddhism) that aim at the dilution of self with the world by primarily abandoning attachment to possessions. Philosophers and metaphysicians ask, "What determines and constitutes the essence of possession?" "What is owned or what can be claimed as such?" "What is it that I claim is mine as opposed to others?" In psychological terms, these questions translate to one question, "What are the mechanisms leading to the sense of possession, the claim of ownership, and eventually the notion of property?"

Developmental psychology can illuminate these perennial questions in a new way, providing some natural grounding for what might be the constitutive elements of possession in general, and claimed ownership and the notion of property in particular. With that in mind, I describe next the various kinds and levels of possession manifested by children in their development. The proposed developmental road map (model) outlines six levels that unfold in a chronological order between birth and five years of age. It represents a natural history of possession in early human development.

Six Levels of Possession Unfolding in Early Development

The proposed developmental model is summarized in Table 3.1. Six levels of possession are distinguished, in the chronological order of their emergence between birth and five years. Associated with each level are corresponding "kinds" of possession (the presumed psychological nature of possession at this level), as well as the corresponding subjective "self-experience" of possession the child might have at this level and the "process" or mechanism determining such experience.

What changes from one level to another is the psychological meaning of possession, one new meaning not erasing the preceding but rather

Table 3.1. Levels of Possession as They Unfold Early in Life in Order of Their Age Onset and Corresponding Psychological Kind, Subjective (Self-) Experience, and Underlying Psychological Process

Possession Level by Age	Possession Kind	Self-Experience	Process
Implicit ownership I Level one (birth)	Obligatory possession (Unalienable and nonconceptual)	Feeling of comfort and appeasing	Preference and orientation: Innate binding and latching onto preferred things
Implicit ownership II Level two (two months)	Acted possession (Unalienable and nonconceptual)	Feeling of agency	Perception and action: Owning the effects on objects and people of self-produced actions
Triadic transition III Level three (nine months)	Exclusive possession (Unalienable and preconceptual)	Feeling of social control	Selective social attention: Attachment to particular people and familiar things
Explicit ownership I Level four (eighteen months)	Claimed property (Unalienable and conceptual)	Feeling of assertiveness	Identification: Self-affirmation and conceptualization
Explicit ownership II Level five (thirty-six months)	Trade property (Alienable and conceptual)	Feeling of gaining	Self-maximizing: Recognition of trade and sharing power
Explicit ownership III Level six (sixty months)	Ethical property (Alienable and metaconceptual)	Feeling of justice	Negotiation: Recognition of shared values

Note. Each level is seen as *adding* to the other. In development, all these levels *jointly* form the psychological variables that determine the sense of possession, including the moral sense attached to it, becoming explicit and preconceptual starting at eighteen months of age, normative and metaconceptual by five years of age.

adding a new one, thus expanding the range of experience and ways of enacting possession. As a function of age, this range expands primarily because of growing social and cultural pressures regarding certain practices that parallel the growing autonomy of the child (e.g., practices of sharing, fairness, reciprocation). Children have to adjust and abide by these practices to control and regulate their situation in relation to others, a situation in which they become increasingly accountable for what they do or do not do. Social inclusion and basic affiliation needs would be the major factors driving such development.

The model assumes that each new level necessarily builds and leans on all those that preceded it, starting with the innate and obligatory proclivity to possess that comes from the immediacy of physical contact (latching on) evident from birth. Each new level would therefore necessarily entail the preceding levels, although these might not be sufficient for its emergence. The levels coexist: the latching propensities and the experience of comforts by newborns or the triadic sense of possession and the experience of social control emerging at nine months continue to operate all through the life span, but in a larger psychological landscape. The model captures the growth of this landscape. Next, I review each of the six levels providing some behavioral illustrations for each.

Level one (birth). Etymologically, possession comes from the Latin word "possidere," which literally means "to sit or to put one's weight or foot over." Etymologically, it is an act of grabbing and forceful physical binding, an appropriation of an object by one's own body. Literally, it is a physical act of power over things. Inversely, and as a case in point, one is qualified as being "possessed" when dominated by an occult power. At a basic semantic level, there is something irrevocable and automatic in what is captured by the term possession.

This is the first basic level of possession expressed by newborns in their innate propensities to latch and bind onto things that are nutritious (breast) or a source of warmth and comfort (soft, skin-like objects).

Infancy research of the past thirty years provides ample evidence that we are not born as just automata, simple "modular" responsive systems endowed with biologically prescribed reflexes. Rather than born lacking unity and in a disorganized behavioral state, we now know that newborns are best described as oriented and exploratory. Neonates are open-loop learning systems constrained by propensities to act as a function of pre-adapted action systems that tap into the resources of the environment necessary for the child's survival outside the womb (see Reed, 1982; Rochat & Senders, 1991). These action systems include feeding (sucking), exploring (novelty preference and habituation), orienting (guiding of action toward meaningful resources), or proximity seeking (maintenance of care, warmth, and comfort). Newborns learn quickly, predict outcomes, and can be selective based on past experience. More than reflex machines, they are constantly redefining their field of phenomenal experience in learning and becoming more proficient in their propensities to act (Rochat, 2001). For example, immediately after birth, infants show more sustained visual attention and orientation to face-like displays, compared with any other objects in their environment (Johnson, Dziurawiec, Ellis, & Morton, 1991). They discriminate and show preference for the voice as well as the smell of their mother's milk or amniotic fluid, compared with the voice, milk, or amniotic fluid of a female stranger (DeCasper & Fifer, 1980; Marlier, Schaal, & Soussignan, 1998a, 1998b). All these facts demonstrate that we are born orienting and discriminating in relation to particular features and objects of the environment.

The selective nature of newborns' behavior suggests that they are capable of possession in the minimal sense of grabbing, latching onto things, and forceful *physical binding*, an appropriation of an object by one's own body. Probably the most telling example of level one possession is the highly predictable neonatal rooting response toward the breast or any other mouth-able objects that comes in contact with the infant's cheek. The infant tends to orient systematically toward this object with the goal of orally latching onto it (Blass, Fillion, Hoffmeyer, Metzger, & Rochat, 1989). The oral latching of the neonate to the breast or any other mouth-able object corresponds to possession in the minimal sense proposed here. Note that this act of possession is selective, as newborns root differentially toward an external object touching their cheek compared to their own hand. They also latch less when the object is eccentric in shape compared to the biological nipple (Rochat, 1983, 1987; Rochat & Hespos, 1997).

At this first, starting-state level, the feeling of comfort and appeasing dominates the child's sense of possession.

Level two (two months). If newborns show forceful physical binding with selected objects in the environment, they do not show yet a clear sense that they themselves are agents of their preferential binding. Evidence of such implicit (still nonconceptual) awareness emerges by the second month after birth (Level Two Possession, see Table 3.1).

Evidence of *owning* as a new process adding to the binding and latching of newborns emerges in parallel with socially elicited smiling in the child (Wolff, 1987), an effective response by which infants start to manifest an implicit sense that they themselves can cause changes in others: the ownership of their own actions and the effects they have in the responses of others. By two months, infants manifest first signs of social agency. The joy they express is more than the contentment we read in the "reflex" smiles of neonates following a good feed. It becomes contingent on the expressions of caretakers who tend to mirror and exaggerate the emotional responses of the child (i.e., affective mirroring; see Bigelow & Rochat, 2006; Gergely & Watson, 1999). By the second month, such smiles and other emotional expressions become "intersubjective" proper, an intrinsic part of reciprocal exchanges with others.

As they begin to smile socially and engage in face-to-face proto-conversation (Trevarthen & Hubley, 1978), infants also manifest an explicit awareness that *they themselves* are causing particular events or effects on people and objects. They begin to show ownership of their perceptual and sensory-motor experiences, eventually applying it to objects as "belongings" of such experiences.

For example, two-month-olds suck differentially on pacifiers that produce contingent sounds with pitch variation that are either analog or nonanalog to the pressure they produce on the pacifier (Rochat & Striano, 1999). By three months, infants also very rapidly learn to kick a mobile hanging over their crib, kicking then freezing to explore the result of their own kicking action (Watson, 1995).

Such explicit expressions of self-agency are not evident in newborns. In relation to possession, infants by two months manifest the sense of their own agency onto things. They come to develop the sense that they possess the perceptual effects of their own embodied actions. They show awareness of an ownership of the effect of their own actions. At this second level, the feeling of agency over people and things dominates the child's sense of possession.

Level three (nine months). By the second half of the first year infants begin to manifest secondary intersubjectivity (Tomasello, 2008; Trevarthen & Hubley, 1978), communicating with others about objects in the environment. They newly engage in triadic exchanges: the developmentally fateful triangle that links self, people, and objects in the environment (Rochat, 2001).

By nine months infants initiate in novel ways the engagement of others when, for example, they adopt a sudden still face. They clap their hands, tap, and touch the other person to re-engage her (Ross & Lollis, 1987; Striano & Rochat, 1999). They manifest explicit bouts of joint attention toward objects, starting to point and grab objects *to show to others.*

At this level, infants break away from the primary context of face-to-face exchanges, becoming referential beyond the dyadic exchanges to include objects that surround the relationship. Social exchanges become object-oriented, literally "objectified" in addition to being the expression of a process of emotional coregulation.

In relation to possession, what is new is the fact that from then on, infants willfully try to capture and control the attention of others in relation to themselves by using objects they capture in the environment physically or by gesturing toward them. They begin to check back and forth between the person and the object they are playing with (Tomasello, 1995), or they begin to bring an event to the attention of others by pointing or calling for attention to share the experience with others.

What is new is that infants use objects to gain control over their social environment, to gain attention from others, and they are increasingly

NEW DIRECTIONS FOR CHILD AND ADOLESCENT DEVELOPMENT • DOI: 10.1002/cd

enticed to share their experience with others. They also concomitantly develop a new sense of others as equal possessors. With this development, the child learns the social power of capturing and possessing objects. It is the power to gain social recognition and attention from others. This corresponds to a third "triadic transition" level of possession that unfolds in early development.

By the time infants (approximately nine months) start to engage in triadic exchanges and demonstrate secondary intersubjectivity, they also start to manifest a new fear of strangers, what Spitz (1965) labeled "the 8 month anxiety." Such fear is expressed by the ostentatious display of clinginess and exclusivity toward the mother or the primary caretaker. Infants start to call for rescue, seek refuge, and are quick to protest when threatened with loss of her attention, another expression of their attachment.

By this age, infants become remarkably astute in detecting their mother as the object of exclusive predilection and attachment. For example, by seven to eight months, infants have the new capacity to discriminate their mother from a female stranger only based on the way she moves her head while gently talking on a video where contrast is inversed, making facial cues almost unusable (it is very difficult to recognize anybody on a negative photograph). They learned the particular motor signature of her head in motion, when all other cues are controlled for (Layton & Rochat, 2007). By eight months, infants develop a sophisticated ability to track their object of love.

Interestingly, at around the same time (end of the first year) infants begin also to manifest a sense of exclusive possession toward specific objects, what Donald Winnicott (1982, 1989) coined as "transitional objects." For Winnicott, such objects of attachment are a psychological substitute of the mother and the control of her presence. Such exclusive possession helps the child to cope with separation, particularly when the child starts to crawl and walk, achieving new autonomous ways of roaming and exploring the world away from the secure base of the mother (Bowlby, 1969/1982). This level of possession is "preconceptual" because unlike level one or two possession that are nonconceptual, it is the source of clear and newly explicit categorization of objects and people for which infants start to have exclusive "fetishist" predilections, commonly turning into "fetishism" as in the case of transitional objects. On the other hand, it is not yet fully conceptual because it is still limited in its range, primarily focusing on the mother, at least in the Western context of an intact nuclear family environment.

At this third level, a feeling of *social control* would dominate the child's sense of possession and "exclusivity" over certain things. Simultaneously, children also learn about others' sense of possession by how they use objects to exert power and control over them in the context of triadic exchanges (e.g., joint attention via pointing, gazing, demonstrating, requesting, offering, or teasing).

The triadic transition occurring at nine months is instrumental in this development. It is at this point that infants discover the power of possessed objects in enabling them to gain social attention (emergence of joint attention and secondary intersubjectivity).

Level four (eighteen months). From the middle of the second year, children begin to explicitly recognize themselves in mirrors; for example, reaching for a mark surreptitiously put on their faces that they discover while looking at their mirror reflection (Amsterdam, 1972; Lewis & Brooks-Gunn, 1979). By twenty-one months, as children become proficient speakers and as the volume of their vocabulary explodes, their mouth also becomes full of personal pronouns and adjectives like "I," "Me," but also *"Mine!"* (Bates, 1990; Tomasello, 1998).

Beyond attachment and explicit exclusivity expressed toward familiar persons, including "transitional" objects, by two years children (at least in an industrial Western culture like the United States) start to claim possession of most things they feel threatened to lose, particularly in a situation where they have to compete with playmates or siblings. Such behavior is part of the so-called terrible twos, a period marked by frequent tantrums and fights to possess things, aside from common stubbornness and the inclination to take off to escape control, monopolize attention, and ultimately gauge their own situation in relation to others.

Level four possession can be seen as a redescription of what happened at level two, but applied to objects instead of actions (owning objects instead of owning the effects of embodied actions shown at two months). By eighteen months, the child applies what he established at level three, namely the power of objects to control social attention. Now, the child literally *incorporates* this power to the self by claiming that it is *"mine!,"* also meaning that it is *"not yours!."*

What is new at this level is that the child explicitly projects herself or himself into the object, identifying with it. "That" object is now publicly recognized as an extension of "Me." As opposed to the preceding levels of possession, level four is conceptual in the sense that the possession is recognized and explicitly identified as an extension of the self. Because it is recognized and publicly identified, possession is now elevated to the new conceptual level of *property*. The affirmation of self and the identification of "Me" as proprietor of the object characterize this new level of possession.

The trademark of level four possession is thus the absolute, self-proclaimed identification of the child as proprietor. The claim possession is *self-elevating* and *self-magnifying* in relation to others. When the child begins to say *"Mine!,"* it is primarily self-asserting, the primary message being that it is nobody else's.

At this fourth level, the feeling of self-assertiveness dominates the child's subjective experience of possession as property, still construed by the child as unalienable.

NEW DIRECTIONS FOR CHILD AND ADOLESCENT DEVELOPMENT • DOI: 10.1002/cd

It is only progressively that the child will develop the central notion that objects that are possessed gain additional social power by being brought into a space of exchange. This is the major progress emerging with the last *two* levels of possession.

Level five (thirty-six months). Based on recent research on sharing in preschool children from various cultures and socioeconomic backgrounds, the transition from unalienable (absolute) to alienable (tradable) possession occurs universally starting at three years of age (Rochat et al., 2009).

The notion of possession, from being by the end of the second year primarily a claim of unalienability and self-edification (level four), becomes alienable and shareable. Children discover the social power of possession in the context of exchanges (Faigenbaum, 2005).

When asked to share possession of valuable goods (e.g., food or toys), two-year-olds often experience it as a loss and a threat. They show resistance. Potential returns or exchanges are under their radar, not yet a considered option. Things change by three years of age. Children understand exchange and trading. However, they start with a marked trend toward self-maximizing gains in such trades (a lot for me and a minimum to others). This starting trend appears universal even if it is more or less prevalent across cultures (Rochat et al., 2009). If children do understand the alienability of possession, there are still remnants of the absolutist, unalienable sense of possession characterizing level four.

For example, in one study we enticed three-year-olds to barter some stickers from their collection to obtain a much more valuable sticker from the experimenter (bigger, much more colorful and fancy). If the child accepted, the experimenter asked her to make a bid. Following the procedure, the experimenter then turned down the child's bid, asking the child to make another one. What we found is that three-year-olds often make a second bid that is unchanged compared with the first one. They do not demonstrate an understanding of trading and what it would take to eventually conclude the exchange (i.e., make a different, higher bid; Rochat, Winning, & Berg, in preparation).

Three-year-olds do understand sharing but are not particularly inclined to practice it. They develop the notion that possessed objects can be given or exchanged, but their motive is strongly biased toward self-maximizing gains.

In another study, we asked children to split seven or eight candies between themselves and an experimenter, distributing the candies in their respective containers. After a few rounds, the experimenter then told the children that they were going to continue the sharing, but this time with a rule change: the child now had to make two piles of candies, with the experimenter choosing which pile she wanted (biblical or "perfect sharing" condition). We found that three-year-olds were significantly more equitable in their distribution in the perfect sharing condition compared with the one where they distribute the candies (Rochat et al., 2009). This result clearly shows that children understand sharing, thus the alienability of what is possessed, but are very astutely guided by an absolute drive toward the self-maximizing gains. At this fifth level, the feeling of gaining dominates the child's sense of alienable possession.

Level six (sixty months). Level six of explicit ownership unfolds by five years of age with the development of ethical possession. The novelty of this level is that children understand and experience possession at a meta-conceptual level. They now factor what others might feel and think while trading with them. Children not only possess something that they construe as potentially tradable, hence alienable (level five), but also that a possession as property can be given or exchanged based on what other people want or need. They develop an explicit sense of justice. They also develop a sense of fairness that they assume is shared with others and should rule exchanges (see also, Blake & Harris, this volume; Friedman, Neary, Defeyter, & Malcolm, this volume).

At this level, children are less inclined to self-maximize when asked to share and consider what might be fair or "just" between themselves and another individual, or between third-party protagonists. For example, we found that children become explicitly selective in how they distribute resources between dolls that are described as either rich or poor, already possessing a lot or a little. By five years, children across cultural backgrounds (United States, Brazil, Japan, Samoa, or Vanuatu) tend systematically to favor the poor doll (Rochat, Lawler, & Berg, in preparation).

Level six possession emerges in parallel with the development of theories of mind when children begin to construe the belief and knowledge of others; for example, whether their beliefs are correct or false (Wellman, 2002). The development of theories of mind is robust and synchronous across cultures. Five-year-old children from all over the world understand that other people can hold false beliefs (Callaghan et al., 2005). At three years (level five), very few children do so.

The development of theories of mind ability is necessary for any negotiation of value in the trading of property to take place. Agreements on "What is worth what?" and "Who deserves what?" can only be reached if the protagonists have an ability to anticipate with appropriate accuracy what is on the mind of others (what they want and think, what they might need, or how attached they are to their possessions, i.e., some accurate theories of mind).

For example, five-year-olds become significantly more flexible in the bartering exchange of stickers, willing to raise or at least change their bid if it is turned down by the experimenter (see earlier; Rochat, Winning, & Berg, in preparation). At level six, children construe possession as alienable but at a novel "coconscious" level that factors not only self-experience, but also the feelings, thoughts, and experience of others (Rochat, 2009). At this last level, the feeling of justice dominates the child's sense of alienable property.

NEW DIRECTIONS FOR CHILD AND ADOLESCENT DEVELOPMENT • DOI: 10.1002/cd

Conclusions and Summary

Possession is deeply rooted in development, as it is deeply rooted in evolution. It is a central psychological issue expressed from birth. I tried to show that the psychology surrounding possession changes rapidly between birth and five years of age, following a chronology of six major levels. More levels could be distinguished based on a different and finer analysis. However, the developmental model presented here points to what I propose are the major changes in children's experience of possession, from being implicit and unalienable, to becoming explicit and alienable property.

The triadic transition occurring at nine months is particularly instrumental in this development. It is at this new level that infants show the first explicit signs of exclusive possession (stranger anxiety and transitional objects). It is also at the same time, and not haphazardly, that infants discover the power of possessed objects in enabling them to gain social attention (emergence of joint attention and secondary intersubjectivity).

From gaining social control they also gain the affirmation of who they are by claiming property at the next level (level four). However, the claimed or identified, hence conceptual property by eighteen months, brings with it much conflict and social tensions because it is still unalienable for the child. It is only at the next two levels (thirty-six and sixty months approximately), that children, constrained by the necessities of social exchanges, understand the additional social power that one gains by trading property.

Possession as property becomes alienable, and this opens up a completely new horizon of social cognitive progress, including the emergence of an explicit moral sense. Starting at five years of age, and contingent with the development of theories of mind capacity, children develop the sense of possession as ethical property. At this final level, children experience possession with the feeling of what is right and what is wrong. They begin to take an explicit ethical stance toward who should own what and why.

In conclusion, it appears that the innate inclination to latch on and desperately try to possess objects by assimilating them to the embodied self (via incorporation) might be the major source of the moral sense that children eventually develop when they reach school age.

The instinct to possess is obligatory, yet it is incompatible with a social harmony. Children transcend the dominance of coercive lion share principles that are pervasive in the social life of animals. Between birth and five years of age, they learn the social benefits of possessing, not just to defend and hold on to things, but to trade and exchange based on a shared understanding of practices and values.

If the ultimate benefits of the ethical stance that children take starting at age five are obvious, the proximate mechanisms driving children in this development from birth remain largely unexplored. More empirical research is needed to illuminate the origin of possession and consequent morality.

References

Amsterdam, B. (1972). Mirror self-image reactions before age two. *Developmental Psychobiology*, 5, 297–305.

Bates, E. (1990). Language about me and you: Pronominal reference and the emerging concept of self. In D. Cicchetti & M. Beeghly (Eds.), *The self in transition: Infancy to childhood* (pp. 165–182). Chicago, IL: University of Chicago Press.

Bigelow, A. E., & Rochat, P. (2006). Two-month-old infants' sensitivity to social contingency in mother–infant and stranger–infant interaction. *Infancy*, 9, 313–325.

Blake, P. R., & Harris, P. L. (2011). Early representations of ownership. In H. Ross & O. Friedman (Eds.), *Origins of ownership of property. New Directions for Child and Adolescent Development*, 132, 39–51.

Blass, E. M., Fillion, T. J., Hoffmeyer, L. B., Metzger, M. A., & Rochat, P. (1989). Sensorimotor and motivational determinants of hand-mouth coordination in 1–3-day-old human infants. *Developmental Psychology*, 25, 963–975.

Bowlby, J. (1969/1982). *Attachment and loss*. New York, NY: Basic Books.

Brosnan, S. F. (2011). Property in nonhuman primates. In H. Ross & O. Friedman (Eds.), *Origins of ownership of property. New Directions for Child and Adolescent Development*, 132, 9–22.

Callaghan, T., Rochat, P., Lillard, A., Claux, M. L., Odden, H., Itakura, S., . . . Singh, S. (2005). Synchrony in the onset of mental-state reasoning: Evidence from five cultures. *Psychological Science*, 16, 378–384.

DeCasper, A. J., & Fifer, W. P. (1980). Of human bonding: Newborns prefer their mothers' voices. *Science*, 208(4448), 1174–1176.

de Waal, F. (1996), *Good natured: The origins of right and wrong in humans and other animals*. Cambridge, MA: Harvard University Press.

Faigenbaum, G. (2005). *Children's economic experience: Exchange, reciprocity, and value*. Buenos Aires, Argentina: Libros EnRed.

Friedman, O., Neary, K. R., Defeyter, M. A., & Malcolm, S. L. (2011). Ownership and object history. In H. Ross & O. Friedman (Eds.), *Origins of ownership of property. New Directions for Child and Adolescent Development*, 132, 79–89.

Gergely, G., & Watson, J. S. (1999). Early socio-emotional development: Contingency perception and the social-biofeedback model. In P. Rochat (Ed.), *Early social cognition: Understanding others in the first months of life* (pp. 101–136). Mahwah, NJ: Erlbaum.

Johnson, M., Dziurawiec, S., Ellis, H. D., & Morton, J. (1991). Newborns' preferential tracking of face-like stimuli and its subsequent decline. *Cognition*, 40, 1–19.

Layton, D., & Rochat, P. (2007). Contribution of motion information to maternal face discrimination in infancy. *Infancy*, 12(3), 1–15.

Lewis, M., & Brooks-Gunn, J. (1979). Social cognition and the acquisition of self. New York, NY: Plenum Press.

Marlier, L., Schaal, B., & Soussignan, R. (1998a). Neonatal responsiveness to the odor of amniotic and lacteal fluids: A test of perinatal chemosensory continuity. *Child Development*, 69, 611–623.

Marlier, L., Schaal, B., & Soussignan, R. (1998b). Bottle-fed neonates prefer an odor experienced in utero to an odor experienced postnatally in the feeding context. *Developmental Psychobiology*, 33, 133–145.

Noles, N. S., & Keil, F. C. (2011). Exploring ownership in a developmental context. In H. Ross & O. Friedman (Eds.), *Origins of ownership of property. New Directions for Child and Adolescent Development*, 132, 91–103.

NEW DIRECTIONS FOR CHILD AND ADOLESCENT DEVELOPMENT • DOI: 10.1002/cd

Reed, E. S. (1982). An outline of a theory of action systems. *Journal of Motor Behavior,* 14, 98–134.

Rochat, P. (1983). Oral touch in young infants: Response to variations of nipple characteristics in the first months of life. *International Journal of Behavioral Development,* 6, 123–133.

Rochat, P. (1987). Mouthing and grasping in neonates: Evidence for the early detection of what hard or soft substances afford for action. *Infant Behavior and Development,* 10, 435–449.

Rochat, P. (2001). *The infant's world.* Cambridge, MA: Harvard University Press.

Rochat, P. (2009). *Others in mind—The social origin of self-consciousness.* New York, NY: Cambridge University Press.

Rochat, P., Dias, M. D. G., Guo, L., MacGillivray, T., Passos-Ferreira, C., Winning, A., & Berg, B. (2009). Fairness in distributive justice by 3- and 5-year-olds across 7 cultures. *Journal of Cross-Cultural Psychology,* 40, 416–442.

Rochat, P., & Hespos, S. J. (1997). Differential rooting response by neonates: Evidence of an early sense of self. *Early Development and Parenting,* 6(3-4), 105–112.

Rochat, P., Lawler, J., & Berg, B. (in preparation). Distributive justice in 3-5 year-old children across 5 cultures (US, Japan, Brazil, Samoa & Vanuatu). Manuscript in preparation.

Rochat, P., & Senders, S. J. (1991). Active touch in infancy: Action systems in development. In M. J. Weiss & P. R. Zelazo (Eds.), *Infant attention: Biological contraints and the influence of experience* (pp. 412–442). Norwood, NJ: Ablex Publishers.

Rochat, P., & Striano, T. (1999). Emerging self-exploration by two-month-old infants. *Developmental Science,* 2, 206–218.

Rochat, P., Winning, A., & Berg, B. (in preparation). Increasing flexibility in bartering in the development of 3–5-year-olds. Manuscript in preparation.

Ross, H. S., & Lollis, S. P. (1987). Communication within infant social games. *Developmental Psychology,* 23, 241–248.

Silk, J. B., Brosnan, S. F., Vonk, J., Henrich, J., Povinelli, D., Lambeth, S., . . . Shapiro, S. (2005). Chimpanzees are indifferent to the welfare of unrelated group members. *Nature,* 437, 1357–1359.

Smith, A. (1776/1977). *An inquiry into the nature and causes of the wealth of nations.* Chicago, IL: University of Chicago Press.

Spitz, R. A. (1965). *The first year of life: A psychoanalytic study of normal and deviant development of object relations.* New York, NY: Basic Books.

Striano, T., & Rochat, P. (1999). Developmental link between dyadic and triadic social competence in infancy. *British Journal of Developmental Psychology,* 17, 551–562.

Taylor, C. (1989). *Sources of the self: The making of modern identity.* Cambridge, MA: Harvard University Press.

Tomasello, M. (1995). Joint attention as social cognition. In C. J. Moore & P. Dunham (Eds.), *Joint attention: Its origins and role in development* (pp. 103–130). Hillsdale, NJ: Erlbaum.

Tomasello, M. (1998). One child early talk about possession. In J. Newman (Ed.), *The linguistic of giving* (pp. 349–373). Amsterdam, Netherlands: John Benjamins.

Tomasello, M. (2008). *Origins of human communication.* Cambridge, MA: MIT Press.

Trevarthen, C., & Hubley, P. (1978). Secondary intersubjectivity: Confidence, confiding and acts of meaning in the first year. In A. Lock (Ed.), *Action, gesture and symbol* (pp. 183–239). New York, NY: Academic Press.

Watson, J. S. (1995). Self-orientation in early infancy: The general role of contingency and the specific case of reaching to the mouth. In P. Rochat (Ed.), *The self in infancy: Theory and research* (pp. 375–394). *Advances in Psychology, Volume 112.* Amsterdam, Netherlands: North-Holland/Elsevier.

Wellman, H. M. (2002). Understanding the psychological world: Developing a theory of mind. In U Goswami (Ed.), *Blackwell handbook of child cognitive development* (pp. 167–187). Oxford, England: Blackwell Publishing.

Winnicott, D. W. (1982). *Playing and reality.* London, England, & New York, NY: Tavistock.

Winnicott, D. W. (1989). *Psycho-analytic explorations.* Cambridge, MA: Harvard University Press.

Wolff, P. H. (1987). *The development of behavioral states and the expression of emotions in early infancy.* Chicago, IL: University of Chicago Press.

PHILIPPE ROCHAT *is a professor of psychology at Emory University in Atlanta, Georgia. E-mail: psypr@emory.edu; webpage: www.psychology.emory.edu /cognition/rochat/index.html.*

Blake, P. R., & Harris, P. L. (2011). Early representations of ownership. In H. Ross & O. Friedman (Eds.), *Origins of ownership of property*. *New Directions for Child and Adolescent Development, 132*, 39–51.

4

Early Representations of Ownership

Peter R. Blake, Paul L. Harris

Abstract

To navigate a world filled with private property, children must be able to assign ownership information to objects and update that information when appropriate. In this chapter, the authors propose that children include ownership as an attribute of their object representations. Children can learn about ownership attributes either by witnessing owners acting on their property, a visual source, or by receiving information from the testimony of others, a verbal source. The authors consider the differences between these two forms of information and how they might conflict at the representational level, leading to difficulties in learning about ownership.

NEW DIRECTIONS FOR CHILD AND ADOLESCENT DEVELOPMENT, no. 132, Summer 2011 © Wiley Periodicals, Inc.
Published online in Wiley Online Library (wileyonlinelibrary.com). • DOI: 10.1002/cd.295

> There is no image, no painting, no visible trait, which can
> express the relation that constitutes property. It is not material,
> it is metaphysical; it is a mere conception of the mind.
>   J. Bentham (1840). Theory of legislation. In Principles of
>   the civil code, Chapter VIII. Of property (p. 137).

Introduction

Ownership, in its most basic form, constitutes a relationship between a person and some other entity that is acknowledged and respected by other people. Owned entities can take many forms—objects, land, ideas, even living entities like pets, or at certain points in history, other people. However, the relationship between owner and owned is itself not obvious or even visible. As Bentham notes in the quote above, we cannot rely on physical associations to determine ownership because this relationship is not physical—it is not material or concrete. The abstract and invisible nature of ownership raises the question of how we can recognize it at all. Rather than rely on enduring, concrete indications of ownership, we must encode ownership information in mental representations to acknowledge, track, and update the relationship between owner and owned. In this sense, property or ownership is a "conception of the mind," even if the relationship itself is manifest in various social behaviors and utterances.

In this chapter, we examine the representational nature of ownership, attending specifically to how children represent ownership early in development. Given that few empirical data exist on conceptions of ownership, our model is quite speculative. Despite some proposals that humans may have inherited certain cognitive predispositions that pertain to ownership (Stake, 2004), we do not believe there is sufficient evidence to warrant the assumption of an innate module for property (although see Brosnan, this volume, for possible precursors in primates). Instead, we propose a developmental model, starting with simple visual associations between people and objects. With the emergence of language, person–object relationships can be communicated in a symbolic fashion. However, visual associations between people and objects remain a potent source of inference about ownership into adulthood. We propose that the tension between these two sources of information about ownership—visual and verbal—explains much of the difficulty children have in attaining a mature concept of ownership.

We make two simplifying assumptions to develop our proposal. First, we focus our analysis on the ownership of objects—as opposed to territory or ideas, for example. Children's initial understanding of ownership centers on concrete relationships between people and objects. Focusing on objects allows us to trace a developmental path for a particular kind of ownership relationship from its earliest state. This choice also enables us to evaluate two different representational models: a person-centric model, akin to situation models (Johnson-Laird, 1983), and an object-centric model where ownership is an attribute of object representations. Our second simplification is to focus on how children understand ownership relationships for other people as opposed to their own ownership claims. Children undoubtedly draw on their own experience with objects in order to understand ownership (Noles & Keil, this volume), but their personal relationships with objects may involve other developmental processes that are poorly understood. For example, children form attachments to particular objects that may be an extension of their attachment bonds with caregivers (Winnicott, 1953). However, attachment is unlikely to play a role in their understanding of other people's relationships with objects (see Rochat, this volume, for an alternative view).

Visual associations. As noted earlier, we doubt that children are born with an understanding of ownership. They rely on their own interactions with the world and with others to construct knowledge about the relationships between people and objects. One very basic way to identify unique person–object relationships is by physical association—a child who sees his father with a briefcase every day will associate Daddy and the briefcase. However, even this simple association depends on a foundation of visual processing. To form the Daddy–briefcase association, a child must first be able to identify a specific person (Daddy) and a specific object (the briefcase). Infants can identify specific people very early in life. For example, within days newborns can distinguish their mothers from strangers (Bushnell, Sai, & Mullin, 1989; Walton, Bower, & Bower, 1992). By four or five months of age, this ability extends to pictures of strangers (Hayden, Bhatt, Reed, Corbly, & Joseph, 2007; Mareschal & Johnson, 2003). Differentiating objects takes longer. In basic models of object recognition (i.e., Leslie, Xu, Tremoulet, & Scholl, 1998), infants rely on the visual features of objects to distinguish one thing from another. By comparing changes in the visible features of objects, studies have shown that infants follow a developmental progression in their ability to differentiate objects using different types of features: shape at seven months, texture at eleven months, and color at twelve months of age (Kaldy & Leslie, 2003; Wilcox, 1999). Based on this brief sketch, infants should have the visual processing capacities in place to form an association between Daddy and his briefcase (as opposed to a briefcase with a different color or shape) by twelve months of age.

Once children can form person–object associations the next problem is when to form these connections. Even focusing on the most important people in their lives, their caregivers, infants see Mommy and Daddy touch and encounter hundreds of objects every day. Encoding and tracking all of these associations would be overwhelming. Infants must engage in some sort of selective tracking to pick out the most frequent and salient relationships between people and objects. In many cases, adults will

NEW DIRECTIONS FOR CHILD AND ADOLESCENT DEVELOPMENT • DOI: 10.1002/cd

corroborate children's assumptions about person–object relationships. For instance, a child who points to his mother's purse and says "Mommy" will probably receive corroborative feedback from his parents ("Yes, that's Mommy's purse."), which would reinforce the association. By contrast, an incorrect referent would be met with a correction or a less positive response.

It is far from clear how often a person and object must be seen together in order for a visual association to be formed between the two. Moreover, simple co-occurrence may not be sufficient. Some intentional action by the person toward the object seems necessary to establish an association. In a set of experiments, Friedman and Neary (2008) showed that two- and three-year-olds (Experiment 2, mean ages: 2;7 and 3;5) quickly established ownership relationships when told stories in which one character plays with a toy and then a second character plays with the same toy. Children watched the stories acted out using dolls and props. Children in both age groups tended to identify the first character they had seen with the object as the owner when asked "Whose ball is it?," although for the two-year-olds this first possessor bias only occurred when the toy was placed between the two characters during the question step. A follow-up experiment with three- and four-year-olds (Experiment 3) showed that the bias did not occur when the children were told that each character liked the toy (in a serial order), but neither character possessed the toy. In these studies, some intentional action on the object seemed necessary for children to infer an ownership relationship.

Friedman and Neary interpret this series of experiments as evidence of a first possessor heuristic (see also, Friedman, Neary, Defeyter, & Malcolm, this volume). However, the results are also consistent with a visual association interpretation as long as we assume that children resist over-writing the first visual association, a possibility which we will consider later. On this account, children will form person–object associations when they see the two presented together along with at least a description of an intentional action. However, more work is needed to determine exactly how the connection between person and object occurs. For example, children may not form an association based on one co-occurrence unless they are prompted by the question to create one.

Verbal evidence for visual associations. Forming a visual association between a person and an object may not depend on language, but children's first words do provide some evidence that they make basic person–object associations. Students of early language usage note that infants frequently say person names when pointing at objects (Bloom, 1973; Brown, 1973). For example, in a diary study of her daughter's first words, Bloom (1973) noted that at sixteen months of age, her daughter said "Dada" when pointing at her father's briefcase. Although these single-word utterances demonstrate the existence of an association between person and object, it is difficult to interpret what the utterance means. Bloom considered this a reference to a "nonspecific relation" (p. 99) because her daughter did not yet know the word for briefcase: she wanted to refer to the briefcase but lacked the word and so uttered the first thing that came to mind—the person associated with it. Once children know the words for both person and object and yet choose to say only the person's name, there is a stronger case that they recognize that a special kind of person–object relationship exists. For Bloom's daughter, this type of deliberate reference occurred at eighteen months of age. Experimental studies have also elicited single-word references to owners or possessors before twenty-four months of age. In one test of toddlers between fourteen and thirty-two months of age (mean age: twenty-four months), children were shown pictures of their mommy's purse, for example, and their reactions were recorded (Rodgon & Rashman, 1976). Several infants spontaneously identified their parent's possessions by saying "Mommy" or "Daddy" as opposed to the object name. Those same infants identified similar objects by name when they belonged to a stranger. A similar result occurred in an experiment where children were prompted to identify the owner of objects from their home; for example, their mother's toothbrush (Fasig, 2000). Children could pass the task by either saying "Mommy" or pointing to her. Thirty-two percent of children under twenty-four months of age (mean age: nineteen months) and 75 percent of children twenty-four months of age and over (mean age: twenty-five months) performed above chance levels.

Infants form visual associations between people and objects in the here and now. However, ownership relationships persist even when one part of the pair is missing. Language development researchers have noted that children's initial use of possessive phrases tends to occur when the person and the object are in the same location at the same time (e.g., "Fraser coffee" in Brown, 1973; Tomasello, 1998). During the second half of the second year, children begin to refer to person–object associations when the object is present, but the person is not (e.g., a twenty-month-old refers to "Maria's necklace" in Tomasello, 1998). These absent-person references demonstrate that, before twenty-four months of age, children can encode and maintain a person–object relationship—the association is no longer dependent on visual cues in the immediate environment.

Representing visual associations. Based on the limited evidence available concerning early person–object associations, one trend is already notable: the associations appear to have a particular direction, from object to person instead of from person to object. In the studies discussed, no child pointed at her mother and said purse. This asymmetry in the person–object association raises the question of how these associations are organized at a cognitive level. One possibility, described by Bloom (1973), is that children incorporate certain possessions into existing representations of the owner. On this view, the "schema" for Mommy expands so that the purse becomes an extension of her—pointing at the purse and saying

"Mommy" is the equivalent of pointing at her hand and saying "Mommy." This kind of representation would accord with Piagetian models of the way in which new information is assimilated into a schema. However, as noted earlier, more recent research on object representation shows that infants can have separate representations of people and objects by twelve months of age if not earlier. At some point during their second year, infants must begin to represent the relationship between two distinct representations—person and object. Once infants know the words for these two entities, single-word references to a person while pointing to the object owned suggest a reference to the person–object relationship rather than a reference to the person schema. It is possible that this capacity exists before children can express it verbally, but it is not clear what nonverbal evidence would distinguish a schema model from a relationship model.

In the schema model, the person is the dominant representation, which helps to explain why objects evoke the person and not the other way around. A different person-centric model describes owned objects as spokes connecting to a central person representation. Here, the object and person are distinct representations, but this "situation model" centers on one person with connections to all of their possessions (Johnson-Laird, 1983; Radvansky, Wyer, Curiel, & Lutz, 1997). This organization has an intuitive appeal—a person's property is basically the array of items associated with that person. In Johnson-Laird's terms, the structure of this mental model would reflect the state of affairs in the world. Further, the central role of the person representation in this model also helps to explain why person information dominates person–object associations. However, in a test for the mental models used by adults to represent ownership, Radvansky et al. (1997) found that participants appeared to organize owned objects by locations and events rather than connecting the objects to the owners in a person-centric fashion. Another problem with this model arises when we consider that adults tend to assume that objects are owned even before knowing who the owner is. This assumption requires a placeholder owner until an actual person representation can be associated with the owned entities. A person-centric model may not be able to support this kind of abstraction as the hub of the model.

It is possible that children use person-centric models initially and then transition to a different mental model of ownership later in life. If this were the case, we would expect children to create person-centric models using representations of real entities—objects and owners that the child has encountered before—as opposed to hypothetical entities. Such a model would enable children to get beyond the constraints of visual associations. As long as a child had a mental representation of a particular person and a particular object, she could form an association between the two in a mental model. This connection could be generated on the basis of verbal information—being told that the car is Johnny's when the two are not in the same visual space. Given the centrality of the owner in this model, if children need any visual support while forming the ownership relationship it should be a view of the owner. We will consider a test for this model when we examine the evidence for learning about ownership via language.

The person-centric model of ownership suggests that owned entities are, in a sense, attributes of the owner—representations of property hang on to the representation of the owner. Another possibility is that objects are the central representation and owners are just one attribute of the object. In this model, when infants see a person and object together, they encode a link from the object to the person and that link to the person becomes an attribute of the object—an ownership attribute. This organization has a logical appeal. Person information can be used to differentiate two otherwise identical objects, just as other featural information (weight, scent) can. The same is true when the owner is not known—we can assign a placeholder attribute (owned) to one object and use that information to differentiate it from an identical but unowned object. In this model, owner information is a salient feature of objects that can be used to differentiate them. Thus, the object evokes that information. By contrast, people do not evoke object information because associations with objects do not differentiate people. Mommy is the same whether she has her purse or not and does not change in any essential way when she owns a new watch.

The ownership-attribute model would also allow children to get beyond the constraints of visual associations. As long as the child has concrete representations of the owner and the object, she should be able to form the connection between the two mentally simply by being told that the ownership relationship exists. Given that the object is the central representation in this model, if children need any visual support to encode the ownership attribute it should be a view of the object. For example, a child can be told that a toy car is Johnny's when the toy is visible but Johnny is not in the same room. She would then add an ownership attribute to the toy car, using the verbal information to establish a link to her representation of Johnny. In the next section, we discuss in more detail how children add ownership information to objects via language and consider a way to distinguish the two models described earlier.

Verbal Information

Learning via visual information is ordinarily limited to the here and now. To learn ownership relationships, preverbal infants must see both object and owner together at the same time. As children begin to comprehend and use language, they are liberated from spatial and temporal constraints. They can create ownership relationships when the owner is not present and/or when the object is not present. However, adding ownership attributes via language requires an understanding of possessive phrases. When do children understand the special language of ownership?

By the end of their second year, children both comprehend and use some possessive phrases. For example, in one study twenty-month-olds were able to identify the appropriate picture describing an ownership relationship when they heard a possessive phrase: "girl's shoe," "Mommy's ball" (Golinkoff & Markessini, 1980). Standardized measures of language development based on parent report also indicate the use of proper noun possessive phrases ("Daddy's cup") by twenty-two months of age, on average (Fenson et al., 1994). Understanding possessive pronouns generally takes longer. Children begin to use the self-referential first-person possessives "my" and "mine" around eighteen months of age, earlier than second- and third-person possessive pronouns (Bates, 1990; Tomasello, 1998). Children struggle with all personal pronouns because the meaning of these words changes depending on who is speaking. Some perspective-taking skills may also be necessary to grasp to whom or what the speaker refers (Ricard, Girouard, & Décarie, 1999). By thirty months of age, most children understand, and many use, all of the possessive pronouns correctly, with third-person references ("his" and "hers") appearing last (Fenson et al., 1994).

The ability to learn ownership relationships through language marks an important attainment. However, children do not acquire the ability to add new information to object representations overnight. A developmental progression is evident in absent referent tasks where children must learn new information about an object, the referent, while it is not in view. For example, when told that a stuffed animal has become wet, nineteen-month-olds need to see the wet stuffed animal while they receive the information to identify the correct one (Ganea, Shutts, Spelke, & DeLoache, 2007). By contrast, twenty-two-month-olds can learn about the change while the toy is out of view and incorporate this information into their representation of the object. Similarly, thirty-month-olds, but not younger children, can learn that a toy has changed location through verbal statements alone, without visual support (Ganea & Harris, 2010).

The absent referent paradigms described previously offer one way to evaluate different mental models of ownership. Given that a person is the main representation in the person-centric model, children should find it easier to learn ownership relationships when the owner is present as opposed to when the owner is absent. By contrast, in the object-centric, ownership-attribute model, children should find it easier to learn ownership relationships when the object is present as opposed to when it is absent.

We tested toddlers' ability to learn ownership information using an absent referent paradigm where either the owner, the object, or both were absent (Blake, Ganea, & Harris, in preparation). Twenty-four- and thirty-month-olds were introduced to a set of toys by an experimenter and introduced to a third person, John, shown in a photograph. The photo was then overturned so that this owner was not visible during the test. Thus,

Figure 4.1. Absent referent task for ownership information. Correct retrievals (out of two trials) of the correct referent, "my toy" or "John's toy." Error bars are standard error of the mean.

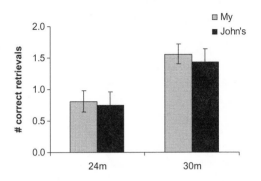

children had some representation of the owner who would be absent when the ownership information was given. The experimenter then occluded the toys from view and told the child that one toy belonged to himself ("my horse"), one belonged to John ("John's apple"), and the owner of the last toy was unknown. The occluder was then removed and the experimenter asked the child to retrieve either "my toy" or "John's toy." Preliminary results show that thirty-month-olds succeed at the task—they easily added the ownership information to their representations of each toy (Figure 4.1). Indeed, they did equally well regardless of who the owner was, the experimenter, who was present, or the third party, who was absent (i.e., John in the example), and regardless of the words used to describe ownership—a first-person possessive pronoun ("my toy") or a proper noun possessive phrase ("John's toy"). By contrast, twenty-four-month-olds did poorly at the task, performing at chance levels for both owners. In a follow-up experiment, currently underway, ownership information is provided in the same way, but the visibility of the toy is manipulated. Initial results show that twenty-four-month-olds can pass this task when the toys are visible, but not when the toys are absent from view; the absence or presence of the owner does not seem to matter.

These results suggest that by thirty months of age infants can add ownership information to an object representation simply by hearing the owner identified in a possessive phrase. Further, at this age children can capitalize on the flexible learning that language allows. They can learn about ownership relationships when both the person and the object are not in view, based solely on the verbal report of the experimenter. The performance of the twenty-four-month-olds also allows us to tentatively choose the owner-as-attribute model over the person-centric model of ownership. For this younger group, the object appears to be the central component of the owner-object relationship.

Differences Between Visual and Verbal Information

Thus far, we have discussed two means of acquiring ownership information: visual associations and verbal reports from others. However, it is not clear whether these two sources of information result in equivalent representations of ownership. One possibility is that the ownership attribute does not depend on the source of the information—verbal and visual information are encoded in the same way. If this is the case, one form of information is as good as the other. However, the results of some absent referent studies suggest that visual information may, in general, hold more weight than verbal information. For example, in the change of location experiment referred to earlier, Ganea and Harris (2010) asked twenty-three-month-olds to help them hide a toy in a room with several hiding places. After hiding the toy in one location, the child was brought behind a curtain and told that the toy had been moved to a new location. When asked to retrieve the toy, children at this age tended to return to the initial hiding spot. By contrast, in a direct observation condition in which the children witnessed the change in location, they were able to retrieve the toy from its new location. The authors interpreted these results in terms of competing visual and verbal representations. When the initial location information was visually encoded, it could only be updated by subsequent visual information. The verbal information about the new location was not sufficient to overwrite the initial visual information.

Differences in how visual and verbal ownership information is encoded in the first place suggest that similar issues may arise for ownership attributes. As noted earlier, children may need to see the owner perform an intentional act on the object to encode visual ownership information. Such intentional action also seems to result in a robust ownership relationship. In the Friedman and Neary (2008) study, seeing a second character play with the toy did not overwrite the association with the first possessor. Similarly, Blake and Harris (2009) found that young children believed that the first character acting on a toy remained the owner even after giving the toy away as a gift at a birthday party. Two- and three-year-olds (Experiment 1, mean ages: 2;5 and 3;7) believed that the toy should be returned to the gift-giver even after seeing the birthday child possess it and act on it. In addition to these visual cues, the children also heard a verbal description of the toy being given as a gift. Still, the younger children resisted updating the ownership relationship, implying that the initial visual representation of ownership was quite strong.

In contrast to visual information, which calls for an inference with respect to ownership, verbal ownership information—"That is John's ball"—explicitly conveys an existing state of affairs. Linguistic information alone should be sufficient to add an ownership attribute to an object. However, because a verbal attribution of ownership does not require the encoding of any action or intention information, this form of encoding may be weaker than visual encoding. If the strength of the ownership attribute depends on how it was initially encoded, children may be able to update the attribute more easily in one case than the other. That is, if visual association results in a stronger encoding of the ownership attribute, this will be more difficult to change. Children would resist a change in ownership no matter how the information about the newer owner is conveyed. Conversely, an ownership attribute encoded via verbal information would be easier to change. Children would be able to update the attribute with new ownership information. If the new information is visual, children should be able to overwrite the verbally encoded attribute easily. Even new verbal information about ownership may be able to replace an older verbally encoded attribute.

Such differences at the representational level would have consequences for children's understanding of ownership in their interactions with others. For example, the initial encoding of ownership would be biased toward the visual information. If a child saw a peer playing with a toy for the first time but was told by an adult that the toy belonged to another peer, this verbal information might be ignored. In addition, changes to ownership may be more easily understood when initial ownership information is verbally encoded. As long as a child does not see the initial owner in possession of the object, he may be able to grasp the idea of ownership transfers.

Children eventually learn to accept verbal information over visual experience in a number of domains (Gelman, 2009; Harris & Koenig, 2006) and the same is true for ownership attributes. By five years of age, children overcome their bias toward initial visual information and accept transfers of ownership that are witnessed and described (Blake & Harris, 2009). However, during the preschool years, conflicts at the representational level can help to explain children's difficulty in understanding who owns what and when.

Conclusions

Research on children's understanding of ownership has blossomed in recent years and new empirical evidence will allow us to draw more robust conclusions about how children represent ownership. However, based on the research to date we tentatively endorse an ownership-attribute model over a person-centric model of ownership. We can imagine further experiments to differentiate these models, such as a child-friendly version of the fan effect paradigm used with adults (Radvansky et al., 1997). The ownership-attribute model also provides a theoretical basis for assessing how the form of ownership information, visual or verbal, might affect how children learn who owns what.

New Directions for Child and Adolescent Development • DOI: 10.1002/cd

References

Bates, E. (1990). Language about me and you: Pronominal reference and the emerging concept of self. In D. Cicchetti & M. Beeghly (Eds.), *The self in transition: Infancy to childhood*. Chicago, IL: University of Chicago Press.

Bentham, J. (1840) *Theory of legislation*. Vol. 1. Translated from the French of Etienne Dumont by R. Hildreth. Boston: Weeks, Jordan, & Company.

Blake, P. R., Ganea, P. A., & Harris, P. L. (in preparation). Toddlers create representations of ownership based on testimony from others. Manuscript in preparation.

Blake, P. R., & Harris, P. L. (2009). Children's understanding of ownership transfers. *Cognitive Development, 24*, 133–145.

Bloom, L. (1973). *One word at a time*. The Hague: Mouton & Co, B.V.

Brown, R. (1973). *A first language: The early stages*. Cambridge, MA: Harvard University Press.

Brosnan, S. F. (2011). Property in nonhuman primates. In H. Ross & O. Friedman (Eds.), *Origins of ownership of property. New Directions for Child and Adolescent Development, 132*, 9–22.

Bushnell, I. W. R., Sai, F., & Mullin, J. T. (1989). Neonatal recognition of the mother's face. *British Journal of Developmental Psychology, 7*, 3–15.

Fasig, L. G. (2000). Toddler's understanding of ownership: Implications for self-concept development. *Social Development, 9*, 370–382.

Fenson, L., Dale, P. S., Reznick, J. S., Bates, E., Thal, D. J., & Pethick, S. J. (1994). Variability in early communicative development. *Monographs of the Society for Research in Child Development, Serial No. 242, Vol. 59*.

Friedman, O., & Neary, K. R. (2008). Determining who owns what: Do children infer ownership from first possession? *Cognition, 107*, 829–849.

Friedman, O., Neary, K. R., Defeyter, M. A., & Malcolm, S. L. (2011). Ownership and object history. In H. Ross & O. Friedman (Eds.), *Origins of ownership of property. New Directions for Child and Adolescent Development, 132*, 79–89.

Ganea, P. A., & Harris, P. L. (2010). Not doing what you are told: Early perseverative errors in updating mental representations via language. *Child Development, 81*, 457–463.

Ganea, P. A., Shutts, K., Spelke, E. S., & DeLoache, J. S. (2007). Thinking of things unseen: Infants' use of language to update mental representations. *Psychological Science, 18*, 734–739.

Gelman, S. A. (2009). Learning from others: Children's construction of concepts. *Annual Review of Psychology, 60*, 115–140.

Golinkoff, R. M., & Markessini, J. (1980). "Mommy sock": The child's understanding of possession as expressed in two-noun phrases. *Journal of Child Language, 7*, 119–135.

Harris, P. L., & Koenig, M. A. (2006). Trust in testimony: How children learn about science and religion. *Child Development, 77*, 505–524.

Hayden, A., Bhatt, R. S., Reed, A., Corbly, C. R., & Joseph, J. E. (2007). The development of expert face processing: Are infants sensitive to normal differences in second-order relational information? *Journal of Experimental Child Psychology, 97*, 85–98.

Johnson-Laird, P. N. (1983). *Mental models: Towards a cognitive science of language, inference and consciousness*. Cambridge, MA: Harvard University Press.

Kaldy, Z., & Leslie, A. M. (2003). Identification of objects in 9-month-old infants: Integrating 'what' and 'where' information. *Developmental Science, 6*, 360–373.

Leslie, A. M., Xu, F., Tremoulet, P. D., & Scholl, B. J. (1998). Indexing and the object concept: Developing 'what' and 'where' systems. *Trends in Cognitive Sciences, 2*, 10–18.

Mareschal, D., & Johnson, M. H. (2003). The "what" and "where" of object representations in infancy. *Cognition, 88*, 259–276.

Noles, N. S., & Keil, F. C. (2011). Exploring ownership in a developmental context. In H. Ross & O. Friedman (Eds.), *Origins of ownership of property. New Directions for Child and Adolescent Development, 132*, 91–103.

Radvansky, G. A., Wyer, R. S., Curiel, J. M., & Lutz, M. F. (1997). Situation models and abstract ownership relations. *Journal of Experimental Psychology: Learning, Memory, and Cognition, 23*, 1233–1246.

Ricard, M., Girouard, P. C., & Décarie, T. G. (1999). Personal pronouns and perspective taking in toddlers. *Journal of Child Language, 26*, 681–697.

Rochat, P. (2011). Possession and morality in early development. In H. Ross & O. Friedman (Eds.), *Origins of ownership of property. New Directions for Child and Adolescent Development, 132*, 23–38.

Rodgon, M. M., & Rashman, S. E. (1976). Expression of owner-owned relationships among holophrastic 14- and 32-month-old children. *Child Development, 47*, 1219–1222.

Stake, J. E. (2004). The property instinct. *Philosophical Transactions of the Royal Society B: Biological Sciences, 359*, 1763–1744.

Tomasello, M. (1998). One child's early talk about possession. In J. Newman (Ed.), *The linguistics of giving* (pp. 349–373). Amsterdam, Netherlands: John Benjamins.

Walton, G. E., Bower, N. J. A., & Bower, T. G. R. (1992). Recognition of familiar faces by newborns. *Infant Behavior and Development, 15*, 265–269.

Wilcox, T. (1999). Object individuation: Infants' use of shape, size, pattern, and color. *Cognition, 72*, 125–166.

Winnicott, D. W. (1953). Transitional objects and transitional phenomena—A study of the first not-me possession. *International Journal of Psychoanalysis, 34*, 89–97.

PETER R. BLAKE *is a postdoctoral fellow at Harvard University, Cambridge, MA. E-mail: pblake@fas.harvard.edu.*

PAUL L. HARRIS *is a professor of education at Harvard University, Cambridge, MA. E-mail: paul_harris@gse.harvard.edu.*

Ross, H., Conant, C., & Vickar, M. (2011). Property rights and the resolution of social conflict. In H. Ross & O. Friedman (Eds.), *Origins of ownership of property. New Directions
for Child and Adolescent Development, 132,* 53–64.

5

Property Rights and the Resolution of Social Conflict

Hildy Ross, Cheryl Conant, Marcia Vickar

Abstract

*It has long been argued that ownership depends upon social groups' establish-
ing and adhering to rights such as the right to use and to exclude others from
using one's own property. The authors consider the application of such rights
in the interactions of young peers and siblings, and the extent to which parents
support their children in establishing and maintaining the entitlement of owners. They show that children, but not their parents, give priority to ownership
in settling property disputes, and argue that diverging models of children's relationships account for these differing perspectives of children and parents.*

NEW DIRECTIONS FOR CHILD AND ADOLESCENT DEVELOPMENT, no. 132, Summer 2011 © Wiley Periodicals, Inc.
Published online in Wiley Online Library (wileyonlinelibrary.com). • DOI: 10.1002/cd.296

The first person who, having fenced off a plot of ground, took it
into his head to say *this is mine* and found people simple enough
to believe him, was the true founder of civil society.
Jean-Jacques Rousseau (1755/1978). *The origin of inequality*
(p. 31).

Rousseau began his writings on inequality with the explicit message
that ownership is socially based. Property rights exist because society grants and upholds such rights and because individuals respect
the property rights of others. The social group thus plays a central role in
establishing and maintaining property rights. Additionally, property rights
are social because they set priorities between individuals within social
groups: Owners not only are entitled to hold and use the things that they
own, but they can also control others' access to their property (Carruthers
& Ariovich, 2004; Hollowell, 1982; Macpherson, 1978; Snare, 1972).
Thus, property impacts the relationships between individuals with respect
to the things that do and do not belong to each of them.

In this chapter, we focus on the interactions of young children and
the role that ownership plays in the resolution of their object conflicts. We
emphasize conflicts because these challenge children's property rights and
because conflict resolution can either reinstate or breach such rights.
Moreover, conflicts over property predominate both with siblings and with
peers (Dunn & Munn, 1987; Hay & Ross, 1982; Ross, 1996; Shantz, 1987)
and children's conflicts are pursued within the social contexts of family
and peer playgroups. Children's adherences to ownership rights, as well as
the extent to which their social groups uphold ownership rights are
important markers of their entry into "civil society."

Although ownership is the central principle governing property entitlement, it is not unitary, but rather a set of related rights. Two rights are
central to children's property disputes and are held to be constitutive of
property (i.e., they define what it means to own something): (a) the right
to hold and to use property; (b) the right to either permit or prohibit others from using property (Blackstone, 1766; Reeve, 1986; Snare, 1972). We
shall argue that in the context of their disputes, children place great
importance on these two interconnected rights. Furthermore, their mutual
respect for owners' rights governs their relationships with one another as
far as property is concerned. In contrast, our evidence suggests that parents are indifferent to their children's ownership rights, preferring that
they share with others even when owners' use and control over their own
property is threatened. We believe that this divergence between children
and their parents reflects fundamentally different views of what children's
social relationships ought to be, as we shall explain later. But first, the evidence: we begin with findings suggesting that young children do indeed
accord one another privileged status with respect to the things that they
each own.

NEW DIRECTIONS FOR CHILD AND ADOLESCENT DEVELOPMENT • DOI: 10.1002/cd

Ownership Rights Govern Children's Property Conflicts With Siblings

The primary sources of conflicts between young children are struggles over objects, but whereas peer conflicts turn to other issues as children enter middle childhood, property remains the dominant issue that divides siblings well into adolescence (Raffaelli, 1997). Although older children typically dominate their younger brothers and sisters, there is evidence that the property rights of both children influence their conflict resolutions.

Our observations of sibling conflict include nine hours in the homes of forty families when children were two and a half and four and a half, and when the same children were four and a half and six and a half (Ross, 1996; Ross, Martin et al., 1996). Children fought more often over possessions when they were younger (averaging twenty-six as compared with twelve property conflicts in each family at the younger and older ages); nonetheless, access to personal or family property remained the most frequent issue throughout. Interestingly, at both times more than 60 percent of the children's disputes involved things that neither of them owned—things like blocks or crayons that were shared property or other general household objects that were not owned exclusively by either child. Although conflicts over things that neither child owned were most frequent, without counting all owned versus shared property, we cannot say that the lack of a specific owner encouraged conflict. However, it is an idea worth considering.

Conflicts over those things that were owned by one or the other child took two forms: in one case, the owner was in current possession of the property and in the other case, the nonowner was the possessor. Both were equally frequent when children were two- and four-year-olds. Two years later disputes of all types were less frequent; however, owners were nearly twice as likely to attempt to regain their own toys compared with nonowners' assaults on toys that were held by their owners. Thus, over time, children's conflict initiations tended to respect the ownership status of their siblings.

Conflict outcomes were also influenced by children's ownership. At both periods and regardless of which child had possession of the object when the conflict began, fully 75 percent of conflict outcomes favored owners over nonowners. Additionally, children in all age groups, including the two-and-a-half-year-olds, were more than twice as likely to claim objects as their own ("Mine!" or "My *toy name*") when they were the owners than when they were the current possessors of property or when they attempted to wrest property from owners. Thus, ownership is a central principle governing the resolution of sibling conflict from quite a young age. Evidence with peers suggests an even younger age at which children recognize the entitlement of owners.

NEW DIRECTIONS FOR CHILD AND ADOLESCENT DEVELOPMENT • DOI: 10.1002/cd

Ownership Impacts Early Peer Conflict

Conant (1991) studied toddler peers who met initially in a lab playroom. All children were between twenty-three and twenty-five months. In this study, the children's familiarity with and preferences for the toys were experimentally controlled by giving each child new toys. Ownership was established by having each child's mother remove a toy from a gift bag and give it directly to her own child. Four toys were distributed in this way, two at a time, in two successive three-and-a-half-minute episodes. In a control group, the same toys were simply placed on the playroom floor, again, two at a time, without designating either child as owner. Then, in a final six-minute episode, all four toys were placed on the floor for the children. Mothers, who accompanied the children, were asked to not interfere with their children's toy play. The aim of this study was to see if perceived ownership influenced the children's interactions. Two comparisons are pertinent: the interaction of children who were designated owners of the toys was compared with that of nonowners, and dyads in which ownership was established were compared with control dyads where neither child owned the toys.

The findings were remarkably similar to the evidence found for siblings: when conflicts came up, toddlers were much more likely to win conflicts over toys that they owned. Moreover, the dominance of owners occurred regardless of which child had possession of a toy when the conflict began. Claims of ownership were also more frequent when children had been designated as owners, again, regardless of current possession of the toys (see Figure 5.1).

An additional similarity between the toddler-peer data and the sibling data emerges from comparisons of children who owned toys and those who played with the same toys that they found on the playroom floor. In the nonownership group, children were twice as likely to interact with one another in play with a common toy, to offer and exchange toys, and to engage in conflict over the toys, as compared with the children whose ownership was established. This roughly parallels the finding with siblings that they fought most often over toys that neither of them owned. In this case, however, the situation was better controlled; toys were identical in the ownership and the nonownership conditions, and yet joint interactions and conflict occurred more often with toys that neither child owned.

Thus, both with their peers and with their siblings, young children appear to uphold the rights of owners to use and to exclude others from using what belongs to them. They claim toys appropriately when they are owners, and have more conflicts over things that are not owned in comparison with things that belong to one of them. Property rights are social in that they influence the relationships of young children with respect to the things that they own. We now ask how the social group supports the rights of owners.

NEW DIRECTIONS FOR CHILD AND ADOLESCENT DEVELOPMENT • DOI: 10.1002/cd

Figure 5.1. Ownership in toddler-peer interaction

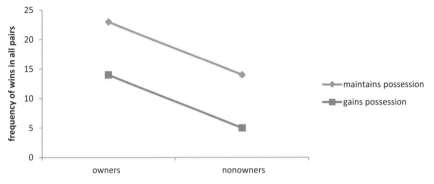

Conflicts won by owners versus nonowners

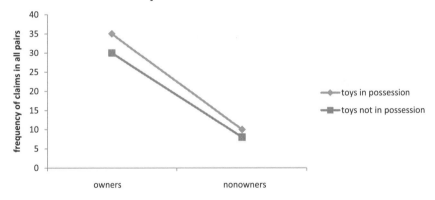

Claims by owners versus nonowners

The social world in which young children's ownership is pertinent revolves around home and family. In formal daycare or nursery settings, children generally are not permitted to bring their own toys to avoid the inequality or conflict that this might entail. When they play at home with siblings or meet with peers in informal play dates, children own the toys they play with and parents' perspectives on their children's property rights are relevant. We offer evidence from two home-based observational studies, one with peers and one with siblings, that suggest that parents do not support the entitlement of owners when children dispute property issues.

Parents' Disregard of Children's Property Rights in Peer Conflicts

Children in the peer study were twenty and thirty months old; they were initially unacquainted, but visited one another eighteen times in the

NEW DIRECTIONS FOR CHILD AND ADOLESCENT DEVELOPMENT • DOI: 10.1002/cd

course of a three-month period, alternating homes with each visit (Ross, Tesla, Kenyon, & Lollis, 1990). Ownership depended almost totally on whose home the children were playing in. Mothers accompanied their children to each play date, and remained throughout, jointly supervising the children while the researchers recorded their activity for forty minutes. We were specifically interested in mothers' interventions in the children's property conflicts, which were frequent and also highly biased. Ninety-two percent of mothers' interventions were addressed to their own children and 90 percent of these favored the peer. In other words, when conflicts arose over property, mothers intervened and consistently asked their own children to yield the toy to the peer.

However, mothers were inconsistent in their support of ownership rights. Regardless of age, mothers tended to support owners in 45 percent of their interventions and nonowners 55 percent of the time. When their own child owned the toy, mothers favored nonowners, but when the other child was the owner, mothers' supported owners. When the initial possession status of the children (i.e., who had the toy when the conflict began) was considered, mothers were no more consistent, favoring the rights of possessors 56 percent of the time. Once again, possessors were favored if the peer was the initial possessor of the toy. Over all interventions, mothers' support was often unexplained (45 percent of the time) and their explanations, when offered, did not tend to include specific reference to the rights of owners (only 8 percent of the time was ownership mentioned). Rather, children were urged to yield to a peer because there were other playthings available or because it was now the other child's turn.

Thus children's playtime in each other's homes does not tend to provide occasions in which ownership rights are well supported by the influential social group. Neither their interventions nor the supporting reasons told their children that ownership ought to be decisive in resolving of their differences. Still, this could be the result of politeness norms of the situation in which mothers were placed. Mothers were likely reluctant to discipline another child, especially in the presence of his or her own mother, and so each mother tried to end the conflict through her own child. For these reasons, we also looked at interventions into children's conflicts with their siblings, where parents did not have to deal with the presence of another child's mother and with the norms potentially associated with being a guest or a hostess.

Parents' Indifference to Ownership in Sibling Property Rights

The data for the sibling analyses was the longitudinal study described earlier (Ross, 1996). Either the children's mothers or both mothers and fathers supervised the children during the observations. As there were no important differences attributable to the presence of fathers, data from both parents are considered together.

Parents did intervene frequently—in approximately 65 percent of the conflicts that involved property owned by one of the children. When children were both owners and possessors of disputed property, parents did indeed support their rights to continued possession at the expense of siblings who wished to take property from owners, and did so in 71 percent of interventions. However, when owners challenged possessors, parents supported owners only 50 percent of the time. In both cases, children's resolutions supported owners, especially when parents had not intervened. Children who possessed items that they also owned won 68 percent of the time when their parents had intervened, but 80 percent of the time when they resolved issues without intervention; owners who challenged possessors won 65 percent of the time when parents had intervened, and 74 percent of the time when they had resolved issues without intervention. Thus, children resolved their differences consistently in favor of owners, whether or not parents had intervened, but owners were even more likely to win when children resolved issues on their own. Parents were inconsistent in endorsing owners' rights and moderated the degree to which children's resolutions favored owners—they exerted some influence, but children more generally adhered to the owner's right to possess and exclude others despite (rather than because of) their parents' influence.

The arguments that family members made as they justified their positions add further evidence that the children's respect for ownership exceeded that of their parents. As we noted earlier, children, even at two and a half, cited their own ownership when they justified their attempts to take or retain the things that belonged to them; parents, even when they supported owners, did not cite ownership as a decisive basis for their support, but rather argued that the nonowner could easily find something else to play with. In contrast to their children, parents also endorsed the rights of possessors ("she was playing with it" or "give it *back* to him") when possessors' rights were supported. When children were both owners and possessors, parents mentioned children's possession rights as often as they mentioned ownership rights as justifications for their support of these dual positions. Thus, both in their support and in their reasoning, parents did not provide consistent information from which children might derive their understanding of ownership rights. The following excerpt of a conversation between a four-and-a-half-year-old and his mother dramatically illustrates the differences between parents' and children's perspectives. The boy (George) and his younger brother (Fred) had been playing with the younger sibling's toy farm, and George asks his mother where he should put the barn.

His mother responds: "Anywhere you want."
George explains: "It's not mine. It's Fred's."

NEW DIRECTIONS FOR CHILD AND ADOLESCENT DEVELOPMENT • DOI: 10.1002/cd

Mother:	"Find where you want to put it. It doesn't matter."
George:	"It's—this one isn't mine. It's Fred's. So I can't do anything I want. He can. It's his barn."
Mother:	"Well, you gotta share."
George:	"I am."

If property rights exist because *society* grants and upholds such rights, then it is the society of children rather than that of parents that teaches children about ownership. The young ages of the children we have studied highlight the early importance of ownership in their lives, but it might also be partially responsible for parents' lack of concern for their children's entitlement. In a final study, we turned attention to a somewhat older age group to see whether children and parents begin to converge in their perspectives on children's property.

Does Development Bring About Convergence Between Parents' and Children's Perspectives?

In this study, we asked parents to identify conflicts that the children had at home, and then asked the two siblings, along with a parent, to talk about and attempt to resolve their differences. Twenty-eight families participated, with older siblings between six and ten years of age and younger siblings between four and seven. Each negotiation was analyzed for the presence or absence of principles endorsed by each family member. At the end of the negotiation, a resolution was coded based on the principles that were included as part of the proposed solution to the dispute.

Three principles of entitlement were considered in the arguments made by each family member: *Possession*: the possessor has the right to continue to play with/use the object, including claims of "I had it first!" *Ownership*: the owner has rights regarding the object because it belongs to him or her. "She just couldn't go into a room and pick up any toy that belonged to Joey and just assume that she could play with it." "No, it's not yours, it's mine." *Control of Permission*: owners may permit or exclude another from using their property. "We would have to ask each other if we could borrow them, and if they say no we would just leave it." Ownership, in and of itself, is often vague with respect to just what entitlements are included; Control of Permission, in contrast, specifies that the owners' consent is required for others' use of the object and constitutes a considerable advance in reconciling ownership rights with the requirement to share one's property with others.

During the negotiations, more than 80 percent of all family members argued that ownership per se should play a role in determining entitlement; however, the children, rather than their parents, were specific about the right to control permission, that is, the necessity of seeking permission for access to others' belongings. Seventy-two percent of the children directly endorsed Control of Permission, whereas only 34 percent of parents did so. Thus, it was the children, rather than the parents, who made explicit the right to either permit or exclude others' use of their property, a right deemed to be constitutive to the meaning of property (Reeve, 1986; Snare, 1972). In contrast, parents were more likely than their children to suggest that initial possession ought to be considered when resolving property conflicts with respect to things that were owned by the children (70 percent of parents versus 46 percent of children). By endorsing possession principles more in the negotiations parents may again be downplaying children's rights over their own property; children, in comparison, continue to strive for control over their property. These findings again suggest parents and children may reason differently about ownership and property and that this discrepancy continues at least until the children approach adolescence.

With regard to the resolutions of ownership issues, arguments based on Control of Permission were explicitly part of the resolution in half the negotiations, which was more frequent than other entitlement principles. The more general principle of ownership per se, strongly endorsed by both children and parents in the negotiations, did not occur so often in the resolutions (only 29 percent of the time). Without further specification, the general claim that one or the other child owned the object does not provide a basis for resolving property disputes. Rather, the specific right to permit or exclude others from using owned property provided a more concrete plan for how ownership rights could be realized. Also of note, arguments based on possession, which were strongly supported by parents in the negotiations, were incorporated as part of only 21 percent of the resolutions. Thus, although parents' views are moving towards agreement with their children that ownership should be considered in resolving property issues, fault lines remain: parents continue to give more emphasis to possession and are less likely than their children to argue for the centrality of rights to permit or exclude. As at the earlier age, the children's perspectives appear to be realized more consistently when disputes are resolved.

Property Rights, Social Relationships, and Some New Directions

Long ago Rousseau (1775/1978) argued that property rights exist because society grants and upholds such rights and because individuals respect the property rights of others (see also Hollowell, 1982; Kalish & Anderson, this volume; Macpherson, 1978). In our explorations of the application of principles of entitlement to children's early property relationships, we have shown that ownership does govern the interactions of young children, but that parents are not a consistent source of ownership principles. Rather, it appears that children themselves recognize and enforce the entitlement of owners. Piaget (1932) proposed that children's understanding of morality develops through interactions with age-mates, where mutual respect between equals enables children to comprehend that justice is based on reciprocity and is essential to preserving cooperative relationships between them. Parents, he reasoned, may actually impede their children's understanding of moral principles. Children's understanding of ownership rights may provide the clearest and most compelling example of reciprocal moral principles originating in the society of children rather than that of adults. Yet we are far from understanding the processes whereby the children come to adopt and understand the rights of ownership (but see Blake & Harris, this volume; Kalish & Anderson, this volume, Rochat, this volume, for developmental accounts).

What, then, is the basis of parents' perspectives on children's property? Why do they appear to be indifferent to children's ownership status? We offer two suggestions. First, parents are not antagonists but third parties who intervene in the children's disputes. We speculate that when it comes to their own property, parents will claim the same rights of ownership and respect similar rights in others. Indeed, it is adults' rights of ownership and the protection of such rights that provides the basis for complex systems of property law (Hollowell, 1982; Macpherson, 1978). Yet adults do not accord similar rights to their children, even though their children appear to claim such rights and give priority to owners when disputes arise. One new direction for future study would be to explore the issue of property rights accorded to both adults and children from the perspectives of antagonist and third parties. It may well be the case that third parties are more sensitive to potential resolutions of disputes that compromise entitlements in a variety of situations, with children's property being only one example (Mnookin & Ross, 1995).

It is also possible that parents and children differ fundamentally in their perspectives concerning the nature of the children's relationships. Fiske (1992) outlined four models of relationships, two of which may characterize family members' views of sibling relationships. Relationships termed "equality matching" entail balanced, in-kind reciprocity, and equality in treatment, status, and distributions. Children clearly focus on fairness: equality is an overriding principle when siblings are asked to divide resources between themselves (Ram & Ross, 2001). Unequal treatment by parents, especially if its basis is not understood to be fair in some sense, is associated with negativity in the sibling relationship (Kowal & Kramer, 1997; Kowal, Krull, & Kramer, 2006). In contrast, relationships based on "communal sharing" are more responsive to differences in needs, nurturance, cooperation, a sense of unity in the group, and sharing of resources that are held in common. Parents may be concerned that their children build a communal sibling relationship based on caring and responsiveness to one another's needs. Parents would then respond to children's emotional displays, and seek compromise from the child who appears least upset by a potential loss (Martin & Ross, 1995). Similarly, parents might expect their children to treat peers as potential friends, and hence invoke the model of communal sharing in that case as well. Parents may be especially primed to consider the harmony missing from their children's relationships when they fight with playmates. In this fundamental way, parents may have a quite different view of a "civil society" from that proposed by Rousseau—one that does not originate in ownership but in mutual consideration.

Broader questions suggested by our research concern the perspectives of family members toward children's relationships as well as the interconnection of relationship characteristics with property rights. Property may govern the relationships of people with respect to the things that they own, but relationships between people likely impact the property rights they accord to one another. Questions of just how relationships and property intersect as well as the developmental course of such interconnections emerge from our findings.

References

Blake, P. R., & Harris, P. L. (2011). Early representations of ownership. In H. Ross & O. Friedman (Eds.), *Origins of ownership of property. New Directions for Child and Adolescent Development, 132,* 39–52.

Blackstone W. (1766). *Commentaries on the laws of England, Book II.* Oxford: Clarendon Press.

Carruthers, B., & Ariovich, L. (2004). The sociology of property rights. *Annual Review of Sociology, 30,* 23–46.

Conant, C. L. (1991). *The influence of toy ownership on toddler peer interaction.* (Unpublished doctoral dissertation.) University of Waterloo, Waterloo, ON, Canada.

Dunn, J., & Munn, P. (1987). The development of justification in disputes with mother and sibling. *Developmental Psychology, 23,* 791–798.

Fiske, A. P. (1992). The four elementary forms of sociality: Framework for a unified theory of social relationships. *Psychological Review, 99,* 689–723.

Hay, D. F., & Ross, H. S. (1982). The social nature of early conflict. *Child Development, 53,* 105–113.

Hollowell, P. G. (1982). On the operationalization of property. In P. G. Hollowell (Ed.), *Property and social relations* (pp. 11–31). London, England: Heinemann.

Kalish, C. W., & Anderson, C. D. (2011). Ownership as a social status. In H. Ross & O. Friedman (Eds.), *Origins of ownership of property. New Directions for Child and Adolescent Development, 132,* 65–77.

Kowal, A., & Kramer, L. (1997). Children's understanding of parental differential treatment. *Child Development, 68,* 113–126.

Kowal, A. K., Krull, J. L., & Kramer, L. (2006). Shared understanding of parental differential treatment in families. *Social Development, 15,* 276–295.

Macpherson, C. B. (1978). The meaning of property. In C. B. Macpherson (Ed.), *Property: Mainstream and critical positions* (pp. 1–13). Toronto, ON: University of Toronto Press.

Martin, J. L., & Ross, H. S. (1995). The development of aggression within sibling conflict. *Journal of Early Education and Development, 6,* 335–358.

Mnookin, R. H., & Ross, L. (1995). Introduction. In K. Arrow, R. H. Mnookin, L. Ross, A. Tversky, & R. Wilson (Eds.), *Barriers to conflict resolution.* New York, NY: Norton.

Piaget, J. (1932). *The moral development of the child.* New York, NY: Free Press.

Raffaelli, M. (1997). Young adolescents' conflicts with siblings and friends. *Journal of Youth and Adolescence, 26*, 539–558.

Ram, A., & Ross, H. S. (2001). Problem solving, contention, and struggle: How siblings resolve a conflict of interests. *Child Development, 72*, 1710–1722.

Reeve, A. (1986). *Property*. London, England: Macmillan.

Rochat, P. (2011). Possession and morality in early development. In H. Ross & O. Friedman (Eds.), *Origins of ownership of property. New Directions for Child and Adolescent Development, 132*, 23–38.

Ross, H., Martin, J., Perlman, M., Smith, M., Blackmore, E., & Hunter, J. (1996). Autonomy and authority in the resolution of sibling disputes. In M. Killen (Ed.), *Children's autonomy, social competence, and interactions with adults and other children: Exploring connections and consequences. New Directions for Child Development, 73*, 71–90.

Ross, H. S. (1996). Negotiating principles of entitlement in sibling property disputes. *Developmental Psychology, 32*, 90–101.

Ross, H. S., Tesla, C., Kenyon, B., & Lollis, S. P. (1990). Maternal intervention in toddler peer conflict: The socialization of principles of justice. *Developmental Psychology, 26*, 994–1003.

Rousseau, J.-J. (1775/1978). The origin of inequality. In C. B. Macpherson (Ed.), *Property: Mainstream and critical positions* (pp. 31–37). Toronto, ON: University of Toronto Press.

Shantz, C. U. (1987). Conflict between children. *Child Development, 58*, 283–305.

Snare, F. (1972). The concept of property. *American Philosophical Quarterly, 9*, 200–206.

HILDY ROSS *is professor emeritus, University of Waterloo. Waterloo, ON, Canada. E-mail: hross@uwaterloo.ca; webpage: http://familystudies.uwaterloo.ca.*

CHERYL CONANT *is team leader, Tri-Cities Child and Youth Mental Health Services of the Ministry of Children and Family Development in British Columbia, BC, Canada. E-mail: Conant@gov.bc.ca.*

MARCIA VICKAR *is a PhD candidate, School and Clinical Child Psychology, Ontario Institute for Studies in Education, University of Toronto, ON, Canada. E-mail: marcia.vickar@utoronto.ca.*

6

Ownership as a Social Status

Charles W. Kalish, Craig D. Anderson

Abstract

The authors suggest that ownership may be one of the critical entry points into thinking about social constructions, a kind of laboratory for understanding status. They discuss the features of ownership that make it an interesting case to study developmentally. In particular, ownership is a consequential social fact that is alterable by an individual, even a child. Children experience changes in ownership in a way they do not experience changes in other social facts (such as word meanings or social norms). Ownership is also an individual rather than a general property; two objects can be identical, but differ in ownership.

New Directions for Child and Adolescent Development, no. 132, Summer 2011 © Wiley Periodicals, Inc.
Published online in Wiley Online Library (wileyonlinelibrary.com). • DOI: 10.1002/cd.297

Why is ownership an interesting and important topic for developmental psychologists? Children themselves clearly think it is important. We know that disputes over property are among the earliest, most frequent, and most intense conflicts in childhood (Ross, Conant, & Vickar, this volume; Vandell & Bailey, 1992). However, ownership is also interesting as an instance of a more general class. Ownership is an institutional fact (Searle, 1995), a feature of the world that exists only through social convention. In this chapter, we will describe the ideas of status functions and institutional facts, lay out some of the associated developmental questions, and explore how ownership provides a productive avenue for research of these ideas.

For the purposes of this chapter we will consider ownership to be a kind of status or set of rights (and duties). People may have all sorts of relations to objects: I may like something, I may physically possess something, and I may make or create something. Some of the relations people have to objects are normative; they involve rights, duties, permissions, and obligations. I may be allowed to use something, modify it, and prevent others from doing so. Ownership is one particular set of such normative relations (Snare, 1972). We will refer to such a set of normative relations as a "status." Ownership is a status; to have the status of "owner" is to have a particular set of rights and duties. Other sets of normative relations may define other statuses, such as "borrower" or "user."

"Status function" is a technical term in John Searle's (1995) analysis of the ontology of social phenomena. Searle characterizes status functions as having a special form: A counts as B. Status functions are defining; they establish an identity. Critically, though, all that is established are normative constraints: people ought to treat the thing as a B. By purchasing an object, it now counts as "mine." To have the status means that people ought to treat the object as mine. There are right and wrong ways people can behave with respect to the object. There are no material or psychological qualities necessarily involved with the status. I may not physically possess the object, or even know I own it, for example. Searle notes that status functions make up much of what we understand as the social world.

One of the significant features of status functions is that the effects of having such an identity are mind-dependent. Status is a kind of reason, a reason to act in a certain way. Reasons only influence behavior when the reasons are recognized. If there are two identical lunch boxes in the fridge, I have a reason to take the one that is mine, not yours. That reason in and of itself cannot influence my behavior. Unless I recognize the status, know that one is mine, I cannot act on it. I might take someone else's lunch by mistake. The status exists whether I am aware of it or not; one lunch is mine, the other not. However, this status has no direct causal power; its effects are mind-dependent.

Existing research suggests that young children may see the effects of status as objective, as independent of mind, beliefs, or decisions. The classic example is Piaget's (1965) description of immanent justice reasoning, wherein the consequences of normative violations are automatic. If someone steals an apple, they will experience a negative outcome, without anybody needing to recognize the transgression or acting to punish them (Jose, 1990). In true immanent justice, even the actor would not need to know about the violation. Adults in many cultures, including the United States at times, endorse immanent justice (Raman & Winer, 2004). Young preschoolers may be especially likely to see status effects as mind-independent. Three-year-olds often report that people will conform to rules they do not know about or intend to follow (Kalish, 1998). The classic false-belief error (Wimmer & Perner, 1983) reflects the view that truth (a kind of status) can directly affect behavior independent of representations. Does the same pattern hold for children's reasoning about implications of ownership? We will argue that ownership is particularly conducive to appreciating mind-dependence; ownership may be one of the first statuses to be recognized as having mind-dependent effects.

The canonical cases of status functions are institutional facts. Institutional facts are stipulations or practices adopted by some community. It is a result of such practices that certain pieces of metal have the status of money (legal tender) or that certain noises/marks have the status of meaning. Searle (1995) notes that there does not have to be an explicit stipulation that X counts as Y. Rather the status function may have evolved slowly out of some preexisting practice (e.g., objects of barter develop the status of money). As a status, the causal power of an institutional fact is mind-dependent; an institutional fact can have no effects without being recognized and acknowledged. However, institutional facts are mind-dependent in a second way; the status only exists by decision or stipulation. A clear example comes from naming. A dog's name is "Fido" only because someone decided or stipulated so. That decision creates a status: "Fido" counts as his name and it is wrong to call him something else.

Not all status functions are institutional facts. People have the intuition that some statuses are natural. Turiel and colleagues (Turiel, 1983) have demonstrated that even quite young children hold something like this attitude for morals. That something counts as "murder" or "unjust" is a matter of principle, not practice. For example, a particular act might be unjust even if nobody views it as such (e.g., slavery was wrong even when it was an accepted practice.) Morals are not mind-dependent for their existence. Preschool-aged children also distinguish conventional norms from moral ones. They accept that certain regulative rules, such as whether it is okay to call a teacher by his or her first name, are matters of convention. Such norms are established by authorized decisions, and do not apply in the absence of such decisions. For example, different schools may have different rules about how to address a teacher, and a given form of address is correct only with respect to the specific norms in that specific school. If a school has made a rule that first names are okay, then they are. Young

NEW DIRECTIONS FOR CHILD AND ADOLESCENT DEVELOPMENT • DOI: 10.1002/cd

children are surprisingly sophisticated about the distinction between moral and conventional rules, and generally agree with adult intuition about which are which.

However, there are several suggestions that young children may not understand facts as conventional. The notion of a constructed, intentionally established, fact is said to be late emerging. Young children believe there is some objective state of the world that determines the truth or falsity of every claim (Chandler & Lalonde, 1996; Kuhn, Cheney, & Weinstock, 2000; Piaget, 1965). Facts are discovered, not made. That something could be true just because people say or decide it is violates intuitive ideas about direction of fit (Searle, 1983). Beliefs are supposed to fit the world, not the other way around.

There is something of a conflict between the positive characterizations of children's appreciation of conventions from the Social Domain literature (e.g., Turiel, 1983), and the more pessimistic views from work on epistemological development (e.g., Chandler & Lalonde, 1996). One difference may be that social domain work has focused on regulative rules (e.g., which name should one use?) rather than constitutive rules (e.g., what counts as a marriage?). Second, social domain work has not always carefully distinguished between authority and expertise. Are the rules alterable/variable because experts are revising their understanding of the truth, or because authorities are changing their stipulations (see Kalish, 2000, for discussion)? Most relevantly for the current discussion, the kinds of conventions addressed in the epistemological literature might be quite opaque for young children.

For example, linguistic labels are institutional facts and often used as an example of a convention (Komatsu & Galotti, 1986). However, labels ("dog" means dog) are stable and widespread. It is rare that a child participates in a new coinage or observes a meaning change. Moreover, there are strong constraints on word meanings. For example, objects of the same kind should receive the same labels (Markman, 1989). It would be understandable if children took label-referent links to be objectively determined (Homer, Brockmeier, Kamawar, & Olson, 2001). Even something as innocuous as a proper name is apparently too serious to be just a matter that people can decide at will. Presented with an owner's decision to change a doll's name from Sally to Anne, young preschool-aged children will deny that the doll's name is really Anne (Kalish, Weissman, & Bernstein, 2000). Five-year-olds accept that an owner may stipulate a name change, and the change is real. Young children do seem to appreciate that labels for objects can be changed, and can act in accordance with renaming (Rosenblum & Pinker, 1983). It is not clear, though, whether children accept that labels are arbitrary or rather believe that labels are defeasible. Similarly, children may temporarily act "as if" a label is appropriate without accepting it as a true label (Kalish et al., 2000; Sabbagh & Baldwin, 2001).

Institutional facts are conventionally established identities, social constructions. As many of the identities we encounter in modern life are institutional facts, it is quite interesting to ask how children come to appreciate this kind of status. We have discussed two characteristic features of institutional facts, both involving mind-dependence (see Kalish, 2005). The first feature is mind-dependent constitution: institutional facts exist (are true) only if people invent them. The second feature is mind-dependent effects: status only matters if people know about it.

Ownership as Status: Specificity

Do young children appreciate that the effects of ownership are mind-dependent? Preschool-aged children are still formulating the relationship between representations and reality (see Wellman, Cross, & Watson, 2001). They seem to have difficulty appreciating that some facts affect people only via beliefs and mental states. Certain features of property rights may make their mind-dependent effects especially evident. In particular, ownership is unique to individuals. People own particular objects, not general kinds of things. Ownership is different in this regard from most other sorts of object or social properties that have been investigated in the cognitive literature. Ownership is like a proper name rather than a common noun. Knowing the ownership of one object is not particularly informative about the ownership of anything else. For this reason, ownership is not conventional (in the linguistic sense); one ought not to expect that ownership is common knowledge. People generally have to be told who owns what, or at least infer it on a case-by-case basis.

To be respected, ownership claims must be communicated. In societies with many identical instances of the same kinds of objects, mistakes of ownership will be common. Such mistakes, or even the possibility of such mistakes, are evidence that there is nothing intrinsic in an object that signals its ownership. Of course, physically identical objects are rarely if ever truly indistinguishable (see Blake & Harris, this volume, for discussion of recognition of ownership). Indeed, we often go out of our way to make objects distinguishable. Children who attend preschool become familiar with the practice of putting names on property. A child's clothing will be labeled, as may their designated space (e.g., locker) and their artistic productions. These marks do not actually create property rights; they just facilitate identification. Children's clothes are labeled so that they and others will be able to see who owns what. With such practices, adults explicitly teach children that ownership effects are mind-dependent; people have to know something is yours.

Children seem to receive lots of evidence that the effects of ownership are mind-dependent. Physically identical things may have different owners. People take great pains to communicate objects' ownership status to each other. In the absence of such communication, ownership rights may not be respected. But when do children appreciate the significance of this evidence? We know that children work to convince each other; they do not expect property rights to be automatically respected or self-evident (Bakeman & Brownlee, 1982; Hay, 2006; Hay & Ross, 1982; Ross, 1996). Do they realize that consequences of ownership depend on people's beliefs and intentions? We know of only one piece of research explicitly addressing this question.

Flavell, Mumme, Green, and Flavell (1992) investigated developing understanding of different types of beliefs, including beliefs about ownership. Three-year-olds generally failed to appreciate that people could hold false beliefs about a range of issues: physical facts, moral values, and conventional norms. The truth of such matters would have a direct effect. Young children seem to feel that such facts are self-evident; nobody could fail to recognize them. The one exception was beliefs about ownership. Young children recognized that people could form different and incompatible beliefs about ownership. That only one person could really, truly own the object did not mean that everyone would automatically recognize that fact and act on it. The causal powers of ownership seemed mind-dependent. One difficulty with this conclusion, though, is that the true owner of the object was never identified in the study. It is assumed that children believed there could be only one owner of the object, but this is not always the case. Nonetheless, there is at least some suggestion that children may recognize mind-dependent effects earlier for ownership than for other statuses.

There are many ways besides false-belief tasks to assess mind-dependent effects. For example, do children think that an object will function better for its owner than for others? Do they think an owner will always be able to identify his or her own property? Does erasing a name or mark erase ownership? Answering "yes" to any of these questions suggests that ownership is not mind-dependent. With ownership, children have plenty of experience to the contrary; property rights are only respected when people know them. We suggest that ownership is a promising domain within which to observe emerging understanding of the limits of representations and the mind-dependent nature of status.

Ownership as Institutional: Changeability

Ownership is alienable. In contrast to inalienable rights (life, liberty, the pursuit of happiness), property rights may be given up or transferred from one person to another. At least in modern market economy cultures (both Western and Eastern; Yamamoto & Takahashi, 2008) young children participate in the alienation of property rights. Children receive property and give it. Young children do not have total, adult-level, independence in transferring property (Ross, 1996), but they do have considerable autonomy. This participation in transfers of property may encourage children to conceive of ownership as an institutional fact: mind-dependent in effect and existence.

Ownership is alienable, but exactly when and how do children appreciate this (see Rochat, this volume, for discussion)? Research suggests that young children may be extremely conservative, denying that real transfer of ownership is possible (Kalish et al., 2000). Young children may hold an "original-owner" definition of ownership in which the first person to own an object (its creator or first-possessor perhaps) always owns it (see Friedman & Neary, 2008). Property may be transferred in a limited way; others may be allowed to use or borrow another's property, but not really own it. Hook (1993) argued for this conception when he noted that young children believe that an original owner may always demand return of property given or sold to another. Other work suggests a more limited conservatism. For example, Blake and Harris (2008) find that preschool-aged children do accept ownership transfers within the highly familiar and scripted context of a birthday gift (see also, Friedman & Neary, 2008). However, it is often difficult to distinguish the limited "lending" of property from genuine transfer. Regardless, object history is crucially important to understanding ownership (Friedman, Neary, Defeyter, & Malcolm, this volume).

In a recent article, Kim and Kalish (2009) argue that preschool-aged children do accept genuine transfers of ownership. Critically, a recipient does not just gain rights; the giver loses them. If children are conservative and deny that property transfers actually change ownership, then they must conceive of such transfers as akin to lending or granting temporary use. If I lend you my property, then I retain ultimate authority, your rights to the property depend on my consent. This conception of transfer can be observed in the context of disputes. If the original owner retains authority, then he or she should have final say in any dispute with a transferred owner. For example, I transfer a book to you and now you propose to write your name in the book. I object. If I have lent you the book, then you should accede to my wishes. If I have given you the book, then I should accede to your wishes. Kim and Kalish (2009) found that young children did accept that an original owner loses authority over his or her property when she gives it to another. Ownership is alienable.

Should children's acceptance of ownership transfers come as a surprise? On the one hand this seems to demonstrate the dependence of a fact (who owns what) on an intentional action (what did we decide)—an appreciation of stipulation. However, children likely appreciate many facts that depend on intentional acts. "Where I am" depends on "Where I decided to go." This is an indirect dependence: the intention caused a physical change (movement) that changed a fact. Ownership could be like this, though Kim and Kalish (2009) found that physical features do not distinguish authorized, effective transfers (e.g., giving, selling) from ineffective transfers (e.g., finding, lending). Other research has found that children accept that intentions determine the proper label or object of representations. What a picture is a picture "of" depends on the intentions of the artist, not the physical features of the picture (Bloom & Markson, 1998).

That children participate in many different forms of ownership transfer (giving, buying, finding) with very different physical properties may encourage them to focus on the intentional basis of ownership transfer. For example, a debate about whether something was given "for keeps" or not will turn on the intentions behind the act. Property rights are transferred frequently, in many ways, and with many varying degrees. This complexity likely exceeds any other set of conventionalized status relations children engage in. Tracking ownership may be the impetus for children to turn their attention from physical markers of status to intentional ones.

Even the conservative results from earlier transfer studies suggest that children accept some consequences of decisions. The recipient may not become an owner, but he or she does become a borrower, for example. One of the relatively unique features of ownership is that people can acquire a new status that is not somehow an extension of another's original status (e.g., the new person is not simply allowed to "act as if" they had the status). The critical feature of an ownership transfer is not that the recipient gains rights, but that the donor loses them. For example, ownership transfers are not unilaterally revocable. A lender temporarily permits a borrower to exercise some property rights. The borrower gains rights, but the lender does not lose them. In this way, ownership transfers may be understood as more serious or real than other kinds of delegations of rights and duties that have been studied in the literature (e.g., Smetana, 1981; Turiel, 1983).

As Ross (1996) has pointed out, parents may not be the best sources of information about the alienability of property rights. Parents assert their rights to objects they have "given" to their children. Moreover, the very notion of individual ownership of family property is problematic (e.g., who owns the food in the kitchen?; Fiske, 1991). In the home and school, a child's status is granted or delegated by parents and teachers. Teachers and parents may "allow use" rather than transfer ownership to children. However, ownership transfers are also conducted among peers and between strangers. Children have more or less the same status as adults when conducting market transactions (e.g., buying or selling in a store). Property transfers are opportunities for children to recognize that their status is not derived from someone else's, and that their decisions about status have consistent and limited implications. Children engage in serious and autonomous transfers of property more often (and perhaps earlier) than other sorts of status transfers.

The Limits of Mind-Dependence?

The argument is that ownership is a context within which children confront the idea of status as mind-dependent. The consequences of ownership depend on people knowing and choosing to act on the status, and the right kinds of actions actually create and change ownership. The very limited review of the very limited literature presented suggests that quite young children do appreciate something of both of these aspects of mind-dependence. However, there is a deeper sense of mind-dependence. A completely institutional view holds that the fact that certain actions create and change ownership is itself mind-dependent. For example, a first-possessor conception of ownership would seem like a noninstitutional view; ownership is not mind-dependent and cannot be changed by decisions or intentional actions. However, treating first possession as constitutive of ownership may itself be mind-dependent, a particular decision or practice that people adopted. The "conventionalist" intuition is that there are many ways people can assign property rights. Some people have adopted the convention of assigning ownership rights based on first possession, but there is no reason others should follow that practice. Different groups could have different definitions of ownership.

The alternative to the completely conventional view is to treat property rights as moral. It just is a fact (a brute moral fact) that the first person to possess an object owns it. People did not decide this; they discovered it. Similarly, it could just be a moral fact that certain mind-dependent/intentional acts transfer ownership. The act of giving is an intentional act, but perhaps it is a brute fact that giving actually transfers ownership. For example, a society that did not recognize the power of owners to gift their property would be making a mistake.

Young children do treat stealing as a universal and unalterable moral violation (Smetana, 1981; Turiel, 1983). This suggests they see property rights as non-conventional; people cannot just decide that stealing is OK. However, that people disapprove of stealing does not mean that they agree, or think everyone else agrees, as to just what counts as "stealing." In a recent study, Anderson and Kalish (in preparation) asked whether systems of property rights were considered as more conventional or more moral. Participants heard about societies with rules about ownership, conventions, and morals that differed from rules found in the United States. For example, in one society, ownership was based on need; if a person had greater need for an object than the current owner, he could take ownership of the object. Participants judged these ownership rules to be intermediate between prototypical moral and conventional rules (Turiel, 1983). Children (ten-year-olds) were significantly more likely than adults to moralize ownership. When asked to make judgments about alternative ownership rules, participants tended to think that it was acceptable for other countries to have and follow alternative ownership rules, but were hesitant to affirm that ownership transfer was actually achieved via those rules, or that the rules could be adopted in their own communities. It appears that the participants were willing to tolerate other societies having differing ownership rules, but at the same time viewed those alternative ownership rules as less valid or mistaken. They held that there are some objective standards to determining what constitutes ownership. Our preliminary results suggest that people do not see ownership as a completely conventional status system, with children somewhat more likely than adults to moralize ownership.

Ownership is a complex domain as it involves a mix of conventionality and morality. We have the strong intuition that people have a moral right to some things. At the same time, we recognize that different societies may have different norms for deciding who owns what. Such mixed cases are not uncommon (Turiel, 1983) and one of the challenges for learning about the social world is disentangling these elements. Ownership may be an important domain for making a distinction between social convention and moral principle just because it is so difficult. The bases and implications of ownership claims are subjects of debate and negotiation, even by young children.

To manage competing intuitions, people often adopt explicit norms governing transfers in specific contexts. One of our families had a "three-minute rule" defining when an unoccupied chair became available. Fair? Yes. But did we ever think this was an unalterable moral universal? Probably not. It was quite apparent that this practice was a local convention, and such explicit cases may be quite helpful in children's social learning.

Summary

After a long period of neglect, cognitive researchers are returning to the study of children's conceptions of ownership and property rights. Ownership is an interesting cognitive problem for a number of reasons. In this chapter, we have focused on one of these reasons: understanding ownership involves understanding institutional facts. An appreciation of institutional facts involves (at least) two things: mind-dependent effects (status) and mind-dependent constitution (stipulation). We suggest that two characteristic features of ownership facilitate children's appreciation of its institutional quality: ownership is both specific to an individual and alterable even by young children. These features distinguish ownership from many other institutional facts (e.g., linguistic labels) and may make ownership one of the first institutional facts recognized developmentally. Researchers interested in developing concepts of institutional facts should study ownership. We think the converse also holds: researchers interested in ownership should be interested in conceptions of institutional facts.

Social developmentalists have always recognized the significance of ownership. Ownership is a frequent area of conflict, but also a matter of negotiation, instruction, and injunction. Children talk about ownership a lot, and negotiations over property make up a fair proportion of their interactions with peers. Recognizing ownership as an institutional fact provides insight into why it is such a focus. Ownership must be consensually established and recognized if it is to have any effects. The way to secure property rights is to communicate with other people. If children thought that ownership was objectively determined, and that its effects were mind-independent, they would not need to be so concerned about getting others to recognize their claims to property. It is only by gaining such recognition that the claims can be respected (in contrast to physical laws that are "self-enforcing"). There are many other sorts of status and institutional identities that children are concerned about: membership in a family, grade in school, or even nationality. These identities, though, are much less problematic than ownership: They apply to classes and/or they are less easily altered. Once established, the identities are more or less fixed. Once established for some individuals, it is clear how the identities apply to others. Ownership, though, is not so easily determined. Property rights must be negotiated and policed. It is (in part) because ownership is such a clear example of an institutional fact that it figures so prominently in children's social interactions.

References

Bakeman, R., & Brownlee, J. R. (1982). Social rules governing object conflicts in toddlers and preschoolers. In K. H. Rubin & H. S. Ross (Eds.), *Peer relationships and social skills in childhood* (pp. 99–111). New York, NY: Springer-Verlag.

Blake, P., & Harris, P. L. (2008). *Children's understanding of ownership transfers.* (Unpublished manuscript.) Harvard University, Cambridge, MA.

Blake, P. R., & Harris, P. L. (2011). Early representations of ownership. In H. Ross & O. Friedman (Eds.), *Origins of ownership of property. New Directions for Child and Adolescent Development, 132,* 39–52.

Bloom, P., & Markson, L. (1998). Intention and analogy in children's naming of pictorial representations. *Psychological Science, 9,* 200–204.

Chandler, M., & Lalonde, C. (1996). Shifting to an interpretive theory of mind: 5- to 7-year-olds' changing conceptions of mental life. In A. J. Sameroff & M. M. Haith (Eds.), *The five to seven year shift: The age of reason and responsibility* (pp. 111–139). Chicago, IL: The University of Chicago Press.

Fiske, A. (1991). *Structures of social life: The four elementary forms of human relations: Communal sharing, authority ranking, equality matching, market pricing.* New York, NY: Free Press.

Flavell, J. H., Mumme, D. L., Green, F. L., & Flavell, E. R. (1992). Young children's understanding of different types of beliefs. *Child Development, 63,* 960–977.

Friedman, O., & Neary, K.R. (2008). Determining who owns what: Do children infer ownership from first possession? *Cognition, 107,* 829–849.

Friedman, O., Neary, K. R., Defeyter, M. A., & Malcolm, S. L. (2011). Ownership and object history. In H. Ross & O. Friedman (Eds.), *Origins of ownership of property. New Directions for Child and Adolescent Development, 132,* 79–89.

Hay, D. F. (2006). Yours and mine: Toddlers' talk about possessions with familiar peers. *British Journal of Developmental Psychology, 24,* 39–52.

Hay, D. F., & Ross, H. S. (1982). The social nature of early conflict. *Child Development, 53,* 105–113.

Homer, B. D., Brockmeier, J., Kamawar, D., & Olson, D. R. (2001). Between realism and nominalism: Learning to think about names and words. *Genetic, Social, & General Psychology Monographs, 127,* 5–25.

Hook, J. (1993). Judgments about the right of property from preschool to adulthood. *Law and Human Behavior, 17,* 135–146.

Jose, P. E. (1990). Just-world reasoning in children's immanent justice judgments. *Child Development, 61,* 1024–1033.

Kalish, C. W. (1998). Reasons and causes: Children's understanding of conformity to social rules and physical laws. *Child Development, 69,* 706–720.

Kalish, C. W. (2000). Children's thinking about truth: A parallel to social domain judgments? In M. Laupa (Ed.), *Rights and wrongs: How children and young adults evaluate the world. New Directions for Child and Adolescent Development, 89,* 3–17.

Kalish, C. W. (2005). Becoming status conscious: Children's appreciation of social reality. *Philosophical Explorations, 8,* 245–263.

Kalish, C. W., Weissman, M., & Bernstein, D. (2000). Taking decisions seriously: Young children's understanding of conventional truth. *Child Development, 71,* 1289–1308.

Kim, S., & Kalish, C. W. (2009). Children's ascriptions of property rights with changes of ownership. *Cognitive Development, 24,* 322–336.

Komatsu, L. K., & Galotti, K. M. (1986). Children's reasoning about social, physical, and logical regularities: A look at two worlds. *Child Development, 57,* 413–420.

Kuhn, D., Cheney, R., & Weinstock, M. (2000). The development of epistemological understanding. *Cognitive Development, 15,* 309–328.

Markman, E. (1989). *Categorization and naming in children.* Cambridge, MA: MIT Press.

Piaget, J. (1965). *The moral judgment of the child.* New York, NY: Free Press.

Raman, L., & Winer, G. A. (2004). Evidence of more immanent justice responding in adults than children: A challenge to traditional developmental theories. *British Journal of Developmental Psychology, 22,* 255–274.

Rochat, P. (2011). Possession and morality in early development. In H. Ross & O. Friedman (Eds.), *Origins of ownership of property. New Directions for Child and Adolescent Development, 132,* 23–38.

Rosenblum, T., & Pinker, S. A. (1983). Word magic revisited: Monolingual and bilingual children's understanding of the word-object relationship. *Child Development, 54,* 773–780.

Ross, H. S. (1996). Negotiating principles of entitlement in sibling property disputes. *Developmental Psychology, 32,* 90–101.

Ross, H., Conant, C., & Vickar, M. (2011). Property rights and the resolution of social conflict. In H. Ross & O. Friedman (Eds.), *Origins of ownership of property. New Directions for Child and Adolescent Development, 132,* 53–64.

Sabbagh, M. A., & Baldwin, D. A. (2001). Learning words from knowledgeable versus ignorant speakers: Links between preschoolers' theory of mind and semantic development. *Child Development, 72,* 1054–1070.

Searle, J. R. (1983). *Intentionality: An essay in the philosophy of mind.* New York, NY: Cambridge University Press.

Searle, J. R. (1995). *The construction of social reality.* New York, NY: Free Press.

Smetana, J. G. (1981). Preschool children's conceptions of moral and social rules. *Child Development, 52,* 1333–1336.

Snare, F. (1972). The concept of property. *American Philosophical Quarterly, 8,* 200–206.

Turiel, E. (1983). *The development of social knowledge: Morality and convention.* New York, NY: Cambridge University Press.

Vandell, D. L., & Bailey, M. D. (1992). Conflicts between siblings. In C. Shantz & W. Hartup (Eds.), *Conflict in child and adolescent development* (pp. 242–269). New York, NY: Cambridge University Press.

Wellman, H. M., Cross, D., & Watson, J. (2001). Meta-analysis of theory-of-mind development: The truth about false belief. *Child Development, 72,* 655–684.

Wimmer, H., & Perner, J. (1983). Beliefs about beliefs: Representation and constraining function of wrong beliefs in young children's understanding of deception. *Cognition, 13*, 103–128.

Yamamoto, T., & Takahashi, N. (2008). Money as a cultural tool mediating personal relationships: Child development of exchange and possession. In J. Valsiner & A. Rosa (Eds.), *Cambridge handbook of sociocultural psychology* (pp. 508–523). New York, NY: Cambridge University Press.

CHARLES W. KALISH *is professor of educational psychology at the University of Wisconsin, Madison. E-mail: cwkalish@wisc.edu; webpage: corundum .education.wisc.edu.*

CRAIG D. ANDERSON *is dissertator in the Department of Educational Psychology at the University of Wisconsin, Madison. E-mail: cdanderson@wisc.edu.*

Friedman, O., Neary, K. R., Defeyter, M. A., & Malcolm, S. L. (2011). Ownership and
object history. In H. Ross & O. Friedman (Eds.), Origins of ownership of property. New
Directions for Child and Adolescent Development, 132, 79–89.

7

Ownership and Object History

Ori Friedman, Karen R. Neary, Margaret A. Defeyter,
Sarah L. Malcolm

Abstract

*Appropriate behavior in relation to an object often requires judging whether it
is owned and, if so, by whom. The authors propose accounts of how people
make these judgments. Our central claim is that both judgments often involve
making inferences about object history. In judging whether objects are owned,
people may assume that artifacts (e.g., chairs) are owned and that natural
objects (e.g., pinecones) are not. However, people may override these assumptions by inferring the history of intentional acts made in relation to objects. In
judging who owns an object, people may often consider which person likely
possessed the object in the past—such reasoning may be responsible for
people's bias to assume that the first person known to possess an object is
its owner.*

This work was supported by an SSHRC grant awarded to OF. We thank Hildy Ross and
Christina Starmans for helpful comments and feedback on this chapter, and also Alan
Leslie for a very interesting conversation about ownership.

Ownership constrains behavior towards objects. Suppose you see an interesting magazine on one of the few empty seats in a crowded subway car. You want to read the magazine, but whether you do likely depends on ownership. If the magazine is not owned (perhaps it was purposely left on the subway), then you may do with it as you choose—you may read it, tear out a picture, and even acquire the magazine as your own property. However, if the magazine is owned, you will not be allowed to take any of these actions without requesting permission from the owner; knowing who owns the magazine will help you direct your request to the correct person.

This example reveals two sorts of judgments that can be drawn about the ownership of an object: (a) judgments about *whether* the object is owned or not; and (b) judgments about *who* the owner is. Both judgments are typically easy to make given knowledge of the history of the object, and specifically its history in relation to people. Suppose you know that the woman sitting next to the magazine purchased it, brought it onto the subway, briefly read it, and then put it on the empty seat next to her. Given this knowledge about the magazine's history, you will likely judge that it belongs to the woman. However, this conclusion is not completely certain because the woman would no longer own the magazine if she intended to discard it by putting it on the empty seat. Hence, even more clarity is gained when the history of the object includes the history of people's intentions regarding it.

It is rare to have this much knowledge of object history and others' intentions. Yet it is typically still possible to judge whether objects are owned, and by whom. In this chapter, we consider how these judgments are made when object history is largely unknown. We propose that a common property may underlie both types of judgments: in both, reasoning operates to reconstruct the history of the object in relation to people and their intentions. In what follows, we outline accounts for how both types of judgment are made. The accounts are loosely inspired by previous theories claiming that judgments about objects often depend on inferences about their history (Bloom, 1996; Leyton, 1987).

Inferring Whether Objects Are Owned

People often quickly judge whether various objects are owned. Suppose while walking outside, you see on the ground a pinecone, an old bottle cap, and a shiny diamond ring. It seems likely that the diamond ring is owned, but that the pinecone and the bottle cap are not. What is responsible for these intuitions?

One possibility is that such intuitions are the output of simple rules that specify at approximately the basic level whether certain kinds of objects are owned—rules like *diamond rings are owned* and *pinecones are not owned*. Although people may use such "specific" rules sometimes,

NEW DIRECTIONS FOR CHILD AND ADOLESCENT DEVELOPMENT • DOI: 10.1002/cd

people must have other ways of judging what is owned. First, there are countless object types, and so using specific rules would require people to learn a huge number of ownership rules, and it is not obvious that people have sufficient experience with objects in each category to learn whether they are owned. Second, sole reliance on specific rules would leave people unable to judge whether unfamiliar kinds of objects are owned. Nevertheless, it is unlikely that people typically have such difficulty (e.g., an unfamiliar tool is owned by someone, whereas an unfamiliar plant in a forest is not). Third, although some types of objects are typically owned (e.g., diamond rings) and other types typically not owned (e.g., pinecones), people appreciate that there are exceptions—some diamond rings are not owned and some pinecones are. If people solely relied on specific rules, like *pinecones are owned*, they could not appreciate such exceptions.

A more promising possibility is that people's judgments are more often based on two broad expectations: (a) artifacts (e.g., bottle caps, diamond rings) are owned, and (b) natural kinds (pinecones) are not. People might expect artifacts to be owned because they are human-made, and making an object typically establishes ownership over it. Hence, a given artifact will typically belong either to its creator, or to someone to whom ownership has subsequently been transferred. Because natural kinds are not human-made, these considerations do not apply to them. Hence, in the absence of other information, there is no principled reason to expect a natural kind to be owned.[1] Such reasoning about artifacts and natural kinds appeals to objects' origins (i.e., whether they are made by people) and therefore concerns their history. Even so, it is important to note that these expectations could also be obtained without considering object history. Many observable features distinguish artifacts from natural kinds (Keil, Greif, & Kerner, 2007, pp. 234–235), and so people could learn that objects with artifact features are typically owned and that those with natural features are typically unowned. Regardless, by having differential expectations about whether artifacts and natural kinds are owned, people might avoid the need to learn a vast number of ownership rules. These differential expectations also allow for judgments about whether unfamiliar kinds of objects are owned, so long as it can be judged whether a

---

[1]There may be deep historical connections between artifacts and ownership. Producing an artifact is typically costly. It requires materials that may not be readily available, and it requires time—time spent in production, in procuring the necessary materials, and in acquiring the skills and knowledge necessary to make the artifact. Given these costs, there would be little incentive to produce an artifact if the maker were not protected from the risk of others taking it (without providing compensation). Ownership offers such protection. It is plausible, then, that the notion of ownership is a prerequisite for the production of artifacts of any sophistication. This leaves open the question of whether ownership is the product of specific evolutionary adaptations, or is culturally constructed itself.

particular unfamiliar object is human-made or is naturally occurring (or alternatively, so long as one recognizes that the object has features typical of either artifacts or natural kinds).

We have obtained findings broadly consistent with the possibility that people have differing expectations about unfamiliar artifacts and natural kinds (Neary, Friedman, Van de Vondervoort, & Karpova, under review). Our study investigated children aged three to six. Children were shown printed photos of familiar and unfamiliar kinds of artifacts and natural kinds and judged whether each depicted object is owned by anyone. Artifacts were more likely to be viewed as owned than were natural kinds by children at all ages, consistent with the possibility children have differing expectations about these two broad classes of things. When shown familiar kinds of objects, children at all ages mostly viewed artifacts as owned and natural kinds as unowned. When shown unfamiliar kinds of objects, children at all ages mostly viewed the unfamiliar natural kinds as unowned. However, it was only at age six that children were likelier than chance to view artifacts as owned. Why did the expectation that unfamiliar artifacts are owned strengthen with age? One possibility is that younger children did not spontaneously consider that these objects were made by people, leaving them with little reason to expect the artifacts belonged to anyone. Consistent with this possibility, in another experiment where children were explicitly told about object origins (i.e., whether each kind of unfamiliar object was made by people or not), even three- and four-year-olds mostly viewed artifacts as owned. Aside from suggesting that children have differential expectations about whether artifacts and natural kinds are owned, these findings also imply that children consider object history in reasoning about ownership.

Despite these promising findings regarding children's differential expectations about artifacts and natural kinds, reliance on these expectations still has problems. Although it may typically be assumed that artifacts are owned and that natural kinds are not, there are obvious exceptions. A bottle cap on the ground outside is probably not owned, and a beautiful leaf on the center of an office desk is probably owned. How do people make sense of such exceptions? One possibility is that they supplement their general expectations about artifacts and natural kinds with additional rules, such as *objects found on private property* (e.g., leaf found on desk) *are owned, low-value objects not on private property* (e.g., bottle cap on ground) *are not owned*. However, no matter how many rules are added, obvious exceptions are likely to remain. For instance, though it might seem safe to assume that a beautiful leaf on a desk is probably owned, this conclusion might change if it is autumn and an open window has allowed many leaves to blow into the room.

Instead of acquiring more rules, people may supplement their expectations about artifacts and natural kinds by attempting to reconstruct the further history of objects in relation to people. In reasoning about a natural kind object, people may assume by default that it is not owned. However, people may also attempt to infer the object's history to determine whether this default should be overturned. The default assumption should be overturned when it seems likely that someone previously possessed the natural kind object, and has not purposely discarded it, but instead likely intends to possess and use it again.

For instance, when a leaf is seen on a desk, people may set aside the assumption that (as a natural kind) it is unowned—someone must have put the leaf on the desk intentionally, and that person's behavior in relation to the leaf suggests the person owns it. If the leaf instead arrived on the desk accidentally (e.g., it blew in through an open window, along with many other leaves that happened to instead land on the floor), then the conclusion that it is owned is weakened.

In reasoning about an artifact, people may work in the opposite direction, beginning with the default assumption that it is owned, while looking for evidence that it has been intentionally discarded and ownership relinquished. When a bottle cap is found on the ground, it is plausible that it was intentionally discarded because bottle caps are of little value and are often purposely littered. It is difficult to reconstruct the same intentional history for a diamond ring found on the ground. Though the ring could have been discarded intentionally, it is more plausible that it was accidentally lost, and that the person who lost it would welcome it back.[2] These examples illustrate that people probably consider factors such as an object's value and location when judging whether it is owned. Rather than these factors figuring in simple rules (e.g., *valueless objects seen outside are not owned*), they are more likely used to reconstruct object history. This is not to suggest that people never use simple rules to supplement their expectations about artifacts and natural kinds; they may, but such rules will probably only be useful for a small fraction of the judgments made.

Inferring Who Owns an Object

Beyond judging that an object is owned, people can also judge who the owner is. Even in early childhood, many sources of information are used to draw such judgments. At age two, and probably younger, children

---

[2]Lost objects are sometimes treated as if they are not owned. For instance, if you find a $5 bill on the ground in a park you might conclude that it is no longer owned, and that you can now acquire ownership of it. This might be justified because finding or identifying the person who lost the bill would be unreasonably difficult. For instance, if you asked people in the park whether they had lost the bill, it would be difficult to confirm that any claimant was the person who had actually lost it. However, suppose the claimant were able to recite the serial number of the bill to you (having memorized it for eccentric reasons). Now you could be sure that this person had lost it, and you would be obliged to return it.

shown a familiar object (e.g., mother's shoe) can identify the owner; at this age children can learn who owns an object when explicitly told (e.g., "These are yours"; Eisenberg-Berg, Haake, & Bartlett, 1981; Eisenberg-Berg, Haake, Hand, & Sadalla, 1979; Fasig, 2000; see Blake & Harris, this volume, for an extensive discussion of children's ability to learn who owns an object via such verbal testimony). Children aged two and older also infer ownership by judging that the first person to possess an object is its owner (Friedman, 2008; Friedman & Neary, 2008), a method for inferring ownership discussed in detail later on. At age three, children appreciate that ownership can be transferred from one person to another in at least some contexts, although children aged four and older have difficulty demonstrating this other times (Blake & Harris, 2009; Friedman & Neary, 2008, Experiments 4 and 5; Kanngiesser, Gjersoe, & Hood, 2010) and these difficulties may even persist into middle childhood (Noles & Keil, this volume). Children aged three and four use knowledge of group stereotypes (e.g., boys play with trucks, girls with dolls) to guide judgments of who owns an object (Malcolm, Defeyter, & Friedman, under review). From age three and a half, children infer that an object belongs to the person who "controls permission" and who thereby decides whether others can use it (Neary, Friedman, & Burnstein, 2009).

Our focus here is on children's and adults' use of first possession in inferring ownership. In experiments demonstrating the importance of first possession for inferences of ownership, participants watch scenarios in which one character begins with a toy and plays with it, and then another character plays with it. The toy is left with the second character or placed between them, and participants are asked which character owns it. Most participants, regardless of whether they are preschoolers or adults, choose the character who possessed the toy first (Friedman, 2008; Friedman & Neary, 2008).

In these scenarios, the toy is presumably already owned from the beginning. Judging who the owner is, then, is a matter of *discovering* a fact that has been true for some time (the fact of who happens to own the toy), and doing so on the basis of very limited information. People's choice of the character first possessing the toy is striking because either character, or both, or neither, could be the owner, and it is not obvious why ownership inferences should be based on first possession. We consider two explanations for why first possession is used.

Acquiring ownership. One possibility is that the first-possession bias arises because in trying to discover who owns an object, people apply an ownership principle normally used in a different context—the context of making decisions about the establishment of ownership over unowned things. Judging who has established ownership over an unowned object is very different from judging who owns an already owned object. For instance, consider how we judge who owns an unowned seashell in a situation where Mike and Dave are walking, and Dave sees the seashell, picks it up, and puts it in his knapsack. In judging which character owns the seashell, we are not trying to discover who the owner is based on limited information. Rather, the goal is to *decide* who has established ownership over the shell, with the presumption that all of the relevant information (i.e., the history of the seashell in relation to the actions and intentions of people) is available.

When Dave picks up the seashell before Mike, Dave may be deemed the owner. One justification for this is that Dave owns it because he possessed it first. The view that ownership begins with taking possession is a basic tenet of property law both in the West (Epstein, 1979) and elsewhere (Lueck, 1995). Beyond law, adults often judge that the first person to take possession over an unowned object is its owner (Blumenthal, 2002; Friedman, 2008, Experiment 3), and young children may also heed such a rule. In deciding who establishes ownership over an unowned object, people's reasoning may be guided by a principle to the effect that the first possessor is the owner (Friedman, 2008, p. 294; Stake, 2004, pp. 1765–1766).

Although the proper domain of this "first possessor = owner" principle might be judgments about the establishment of ownership over unowned things, people might apply the rule more generally. They might apply the principle *whenever* they make ownership judgments, and hence use it when trying to discover who owns an already owned object. This would explain why people choose the first possessor in situations where one child plays with a toy, and then another child plays with it—the child who plays with the toy first is the first (known) possessor of the toy. Thus, people might choose the first possessor because they extend a first possession rule, originally developed for reasoning about the establishment of ownership over unowned things, beyond its proper domain.

This explanation requires that people's decisions about the establishment of ownership are, in fact, based on a first-possession rule. However, recent findings suggest that people may not adhere to such a rule. Although people often judge that the first person to possess an object establishes ownership over it, there are many situations where they do not. For instance, consider the following scenario:

> High above the ground, a gem juts out of a cliff wall. Mike is trying to climb the cliff to get the gem. He is having great difficulty climbing, and the gem is far above him. Mike throws a rock at the gem, causing it to fall to the base of the cliff. Dave is walking by, and has seen all of this. Dave picks up the gem. Mike quickly climbs down, and they argue about who gets to keep the gem.

Who does the gem belong to? Most adults judge that Mike is the owner, even though Dave possesses it first. This finding is consistent with the alternative view that people typically make judgments about the establishment of ownership over unowned things by favoring the person who,

NEW DIRECTIONS FOR CHILD AND ADOLESCENT DEVELOPMENT • DOI: 10.1002/cd

in intentionally pursuing an object, was *necessary* for its ultimate possession (Friedman, 2010). Though Mike was not first to possess the gem, he was *probably* necessary for it to be possessed—if he had not dislodged the gem, it might still be stuck high on the cliff. It would be difficult to claim that Dave was somehow also necessary, because if he had not picked up the gem, Mike surely would have. Judging ownership in this way often leads first possessors to be identified as owners (because first possessors are typically necessary for possession). However, most important for current purposes, it is unlikely that people adhere to a simple first-possession rule in deciding who ought to own an object.

Reconstructing history. To set the stage for the explanation we favor regarding why people choose the first possessor when trying to discover who owns an already owned object, it is helpful to consider some examples of everyday ownership judgments.

Suppose you run into your friend Susan, and she is holding a beautiful edition of your favorite book. You will probably assume the book belongs to Susan. Assuming ownership in such situations is *crucial.* If you did not assume that Susan owns the book, then you would have the same attitude toward it as you do toward the magazine on the empty subway seat, and you might seriously wonder whether it is owned at all, and by whom. If Susan set the book down and a stranger tried to take it, you would have little reason to stop the stranger or mention that it belongs to Susan. Problems would arise if Susan decided to give you the book as a gift, or if you wanted to buy it from her—if Susan were not the owner, then you could not acquire ownership of the book from her.[3] If people seriously doubted that such possession signals ownership, then ownership could not function because it would constantly be called into doubt.

Susan's possession of the book suggests that she *earlier* obtained it through some legitimate means of acquiring ownership (e.g., she bought it or received it as a gift). Hence, the conclusion that she owns it would be overturned if you discover that she did not obtain the book in a legitimate way—if, for instance, she had stolen it from a store. You might also overturn your conclusion that she owns the book if you saw her find it on a park bench. Here you would likely judge that the book was already owned when Susan found it, and still has the same owner now. It probably belongs to the person who forgot it on the bench—the person who possessed the book in the past. That is, you assume that that person, who previously possessed the object, owns it, and earlier legitimately acquired ownership of it.

---

[3]If nonowners could transfer ownership, then ownership would become meaningless. The main function of ownership (perhaps) is to protect owners' access to their property. However, if you could take ownership of Susan's book whenever you chose (i.e., transferring ownership to yourself), then her access to it would not actually be protected, which would be tantamount to her not owning it.

These examples suggest that in trying to discover who owns an already owned object, people typically assume that a person who possesses the object owns it, and that this person acquired ownership legitimately at some earlier time. However, this assumption is called into question when it is doubtful that the possessor earlier acquired the object in a way that legitimately transfers or establishes ownership. When this assumption is called into question, the next best guess is that the owner is whichever person possessed it still earlier—perhaps that prior possessor earlier acquired ownership legitimately.

In this account, reasoning about ownership involves reconstructing history. Current possession of an object is used to infer ownership because it supports the assumption that the possessor had the object in the past, and likely legitimately acquired ownership at an earlier time. When this assumption about the possessor is cast into doubt, an earlier possessor (even if this person's identity is unknown) is assumed to be the true owner.

This "reconstructing history" account explains why people choose the first possessor when inferring ownership in scenarios where one character begins with a toy and plays with it, and then another character plays with it. Suppose a girl plays with a ball, and then a boy plays with it. Although both children possess the ball in the scenario, the boy's possession of the ball does not suggest that he possessed the ball before the scenario began, and earlier acquired it in a way legitimately conferring ownership. There is no mention of ownership being transferred or acquired in the scenario, and the girl possessed the ball before he did. In contrast, the girl starts with the ball, implying that she possessed it before the scenario began, and that she may have earlier acquired it in a way that legitimately establishes ownership. First possession often provides hints about history; subsequent possession does not.

According to the "reconstructing history" account, the girl is chosen as the owner because her first possession of the ball is informative about the past, or at least indicates that she possessed the ball in the past, and hence can be assumed to have earlier acquired ownership of it legitimately. However, there are circumstances where first possession is not informative in this way. A unique prediction of the "reconstructing history" account is that people should be less likely to infer ownership from first possession in such situations. Suppose the ball is first seen on the ground unpossessed, with the girl and boy then each playing with it in turn. Although the girl is again the first possessor, it is impossible to infer whether she possessed it before the scenario began (much as seeing Susan find the book does not allow you to infer that she had ever possessed it before). Because first possession is uninformative about prior possession here, it should not be used to infer ownership.

Findings from preschoolers support this prediction (Friedman, Neary, Defeyter, and Malcolm, in preparation). As noted earlier, children and adults mostly choose the first possessor as owner in scenarios where one character begins with a toy and plays with it, and then another character plays with it. However, four- and five-year-olds only choose the first possessor at chance levels in scenarios that differ in only one detail—rather than beginning with the first possessor, the toy starts between the characters, before the characters each play with it. These findings are predicted by the "reconstructing history" account, but conflict with the view that children attribute ownership by applying a general *first possessor = owner* rule. If children applied such a rule, they would choose the character who first possesses the ball, regardless of whether the ball begins with this character or begins between the characters. (We believe the findings also conflict with another explanation for the first-possession bias offered by Blake & Harris, this volume.)

Summary

We have outlined accounts of how people judge whether an object is owned and, if so, by whom. The basic claim of our account is that when object history is unknown, reasoning operates to reconstruct this history. This method of making ownership judgments is warranted because the facts of whether a particular object is owned, and by whom, typically depend on the history of the object in relation to people.

References

Blake, P., & Harris, P. L. (2009). Children's understanding of ownership transfers. *Cognitive Development, 24*, 133–145.
Blake, P. R., & Harris, P. L. (2011). Early representations of ownership. In H. Ross & O. Friedman (Eds.), *Origins of ownership of property. New Directions for Child and Adolescent Development, 132*, 39–52.
Bloom, P. (1996). Intention, history, and artifact concepts. *Cognition, 60*, 1–29.
Blumenthal, J. A. (2002, March). *Lay perceptions of property and nuisance: Do intuitions match legal doctrine?* Poster presented at the American Psychology-Law Society Conference, Austin, TX.
Eisenberg-Berg, N., Haake, R., Hand, M., & Sadalla, E. (1979). Effects of instructions concerning ownership of a toy on preschoolers sharing and defensive behaviors. *Developmental Psychology, 15*, 460–461.
Eisenberg-Berg, N., Haake, R. J., & Bartlett, K. (1981). The effects of possession and ownership on the sharing and proprietary behaviors of preschool children. *Merrill-Palmer Quarterly, 27*, 61–68.
Epstein, R. A. (1979). Possession as the root of title. *Georgia Law Review, 13*, 1221–1243.
Fasig, L. G. (2000). Toddlers' understanding of ownership: Implications for self-concept development. *Social Development, 9*, 370–382.
Friedman, O. (2008). First possession: An assumption guiding inferences about who owns what. *Psychonomic Bulletin & Review, 15*, 290–295.
Friedman, O. (2010). Necessary for possession: How people reason about the acquisition of ownership. *Personality and Social Psychology Bulletin, 36, 1161–1169.*
Friedman, O., & Neary, K. R. (2008). Determining who owns what: Do children infer ownership from first possession? *Cognition, 107*, 829–849.

Friedman, O., Neary, K. R., Defeyter, M. A., & Malcolm, S. L. (in preparation). First possession, object history, and ownership.

Kanngiesser, P., Gjersoe, N. L., & Hood, B. M. (2010). Transfer of property ownership following creative labour in preschool children and adults. *Psychological Science, 21*, 1236–1241.

Keil, F. C., Greif, M. L., & Kerner, R. S. (2007). A world apart: How concepts of the constructed world are different in representation and in development. In S. Laurence & E. Margolis (Eds.), *Creations of the mind: Theories of artifacts and their representation*. New York, NY: Oxford University Press.

Leyton, M. (1987). Inferring causal history from shape. *Cognitive Science, 13*, 357–387.

Lueck, D. (1995). The rule of first possession and the design of law. *Journal of Law and Economics, 38*, 393–436.

Malcolm, S. L., Defeyter, M. A., & Friedman, O. (under review). Children and adults use sex- and age-stereotypes in ownership judgments.

Neary, K. R., Friedman, O., & Burnstein, C. L. (2009). Preschoolers infer ownership from "control of permission." *Developmental Psychology, 45*, 873–876.

Neary, K. R., Friedman, O., Van de Vondervoort, J., & Karpova, O. (under review). Artifacts and natural kinds: Children's judgments about whether objects are owned.

Noles, N. S., & Keil, F. C. (2011). Exploring ownership in a developmental context. In H. Ross & O. Friedman (Eds.), *Origins of ownership of property. New Directions for Child and Adolescent Development, 132*, 91–103.

Stake, J. E. (2004). The property 'instinct.' *Philosophical Transactions of the Royal Society B: Biological Sciences, 359*, 1763–1774.

ORI FRIEDMAN *is associate professor of psychology, University of Waterloo, Waterloo, ON, Canada. E-mail: friedman@uwaterloo.ca.*

KAREN R. NEARY *is a PhD candidate, University of Waterloo, Waterloo, ON, Canada. E-mail: kneary@uwaterloo.ca.*

MARGARET A. DEFEYTER *is senior lecturer, Department of Psychology, Northumbria University, Newcastle upon Tyne, UK. E-mail: greta.defeyter @northumbria.ac.uk.*

SARAH L. MALCOLM *is a PhD candidate, Department of Psychology, Northumbria University, Newcastle upon Tyne, UK. E-mail: sarah.l.malcolm @northumbria.ac.uk.*

Noles, N. S., & Keil, F. C. (2011). Exploring ownership in a developmental context. In H. Ross & O. Friedman (Eds.), *Origins of ownership of property. New Directions for Child and Adolescent Development, 132,* 91–103.

8

Exploring Ownership in a Developmental Context

Nicholaus S. Noles, Frank C. Keil

Abstract

Ownership and economic behaviors are highly salient elements of the human social landscape. Indeed, the human world is literally constructed of property. Individuals perceive and manipulate a complex web of people and property that is largely invisible and abstract. In this chapter, the authors focus on drawing together information from a variety of disciplines, including legal theory, philosophy, psychology, and economics, to begin creating a coherent picture of the cognitive architecture that underlies ownership concepts. In doing so, the authors review theories of ownership and discuss recent research that highlights the unique contributions garnered by studying ownership in a developmental context.

New Directions for Child and Adolescent Development, no. 132, Summer 2011 © Wiley Periodicals, Inc.
Published online in Wiley Online Library (wileyonlinelibrary.com). • DOI: 10.1002/cd.299

Humans inhabit a world densely populated with a massive variety of property. In addition to "real" property (i.e., land), objects, ideas, endeavors, songs, space, resources, stories, and symbols are all property. In addition, determinations of property ownership are essential to our ability to navigate and act effectively on our physical and social environment. Notions of ownership are therefore central to the everyday lives of virtually all individuals. Yet, calculations of ownership can be subtle and complex: ownership is both invisible and abstract. Ownership does not require a physical or visible link, and although ownership is buttressed by simple heuristics (e.g., the first person that we see in possession of an object is likely to be its owner; see Friedman, 2008), brute association between owner and property certainly does not comprehensively explain ownership concepts in adults (e.g., when someone sits in a chair, it does not necessarily mean that they own it), but the development of ownership concepts may begin with these simple associations (see Blake & Harris, this volume). Ownership is paradoxically both complex and simple. The links between people and property are simultaneously salient and invisible. Also, while the world is "rife with property disputes, at all levels of social organization . . . it is remarkable how very few disputes and disruptions there actually are relative to the ubiquitousness of property norms . . . everywhere we go, everything we do, entails at least a momentary calculation of possessory relationships and rights" (Rudmin, 1991, p. 85).

This chapter focuses on the relationships between people and property at the level of individuals and very small groups, not in terms of larger economic systems or models. Personal relationships between individuals and their property may have important consequences for each person's self-image and self-esteem (see Belk, 1988). For example, owning a Viking range or Sub Zero refrigerator may yield changes in self-evaluations in upwardly mobile middle-class couples, at least on a temporary basis (although the lasting benefits of owning such possessions is less clear; see Frank, 2000). Possessions also provide both instrumental value (e.g., a hammer enables driving a nail) and symbolic value (e.g., a picture reminds the viewer of good memories or personal success; see Dittmar, 1991). In economic contexts, personal ownership can influence value judgments. Individuals attribute greater value to objects that they own, and relatively devalue identical objects owned by others (i.e., the Endowment Effect; see Kahneman, Knetsch, & Thaler, 1990, Thaler, 1980). In this respect, children are much like adults, demonstrating the same rational (Harbaugh, Krause, & Berry, 2001) and irrational biases (e.g., the Endowment Effect; see Harbaugh, Krause, & Vesterlund, 2001).

Owner–property relationships are perhaps most salient in small groups, involving two or more people and their property. If the property rights of only one person are considered, then there can be no donations, thefts, or exclusions of ownership rights to some individuals or groups. However, if more than one individual is present, property disputes are likely to occur. For example, in childhood, if only one child is present, then there are few property disputes. However, if more than one child is present, conflicts over property are quite common (e.g., Hay & Ross, 1982). Ownership is also useful for purposes beyond determining who owns what. Links between people and property can be used to convey information, such as social and economic status, race (Dittmar, 1992, 1994), and gender (Dittmar, 1991). Thus, learning to navigate a social and physical environment constructed of links between people and property is an important task with huge dividends not just in terms of potential physical resources but also in terms of information about others.

Although ownership has been explored across a variety of topics and populations, including children (e.g., Fasig, 2000; Furby, 1991; Ross, 1996), adults (e.g., Prentice, 1987), and elderly individuals (e.g., Cram & Paton, 1993; Kamptner, 1991), relatively few studies have explored how concepts of ownership develop. Developmental approaches are especially useful in addressing questions about concepts of ownership because they help uncover more foundational aspects of ownership from those that are gradually internalized from the culture at large. This chapter focuses on three questions: What is property? Who or what are owners? What are the rules that govern property transfers? These three questions have been largely ignored in studies of child development (with the exception of question three, which has begun to receive attention in recent publications), but these questions represent core elements of ownership. By exploring these questions, investigators can begin to characterize the development of the cognitive architecture that underlies ownership concepts.

Theories of Ownership

Although several studies have examined aspects of ownership, cognitive scientists have proposed relatively few overarching theories of ownership, including two theories presented in this volume (see Blake & Harris, this volume; Rochat, this volume). Even so, compared with theories of property, theories of ownership are relatively abundant. Associative or "single-link" theories of ownership are perhaps the oldest. Although not precisely referred to in associative terms, philosophers including Locke, Hume, Grotius, Pufendorf, and their intellectual progeny (for a review, see Buckle, 1991) use a rough analogue of associative theories of learning links between properties and kinds, describing ownership as a link between person and property that is strengthened by repeated observations of that person in some manner of proximity (e.g., spatial or temporal or both) to that property. Leon Litwinski's theories (for a review, see Rudmin, 1990) supported a single-link framework, positing that ownership is an associative process, connecting owner and property through frequency-driven processes that allow individuals to efficiently keep track of who owns what. Moreover, such a strategy has some utility as people often do own things that they are most frequently associated with (although certainly not always—few people think the supermarket clerk owns her cash register, the student owns his classroom desk, or the prisoner owns his jail). At first glance, some studies may seem to support a single-link framework. For example, Friedman (2008) found that both adults and children (Friedman & Neary, 2008) employ a "first possessor" heuristic in identifying property owners. However, this heuristic need not be associative and could, in fact, be counter associative if it were the case that first possessor links trumped more frequent later possession links. In real life, first possessor relations and frequency are often confounded, but when they are disentangled, frequency seems to be less central to ownership intuitions.

Because individuals do perceive strong associations between people and property, the single-link framework is appealing in its simplicity; however, legal experts and philosophers claim that, in practice, people in their daily lives do not usually treat ownership as a single link. In the early 1900s, Wesley Hohfeld (1913, 1917) noted that legal and practical definitions of ownership gradually shifted from a unitary, single link between person and property into a bundle of independent, separable property rights. This "rights bundle" framework is best described by the philosopher Frank Snare (1972). Snare posits that ownership is represented by a Hohfeldian rights bundle representing a host of legal rights and obligations. In psychological terms, these rights can be roughly reduced to three elements, including the right to use one's property, the right to restrict others from accessing one's property, and the right to transfer one's property into the possession of other individuals (see Ross, Conant, & Vikar, this volume, for a discussion regarding how children might acquire these rights constructs). Critically, each property right does not have to belong to the same person. For example, many movie tickets are nontransferable; the owner of the ticket may not resell the ticket for use as a ticket or otherwise give it away for that purpose. However, the owner of the ticket may still use it and he or she has the right to keep others from using it. Most modern legal systems employ Hohfeldian rights bundles, but it is not clear whether modern concepts of ownership are influenced by legal definitions or if legal definitions are based on prior behavioral precedents. Thus, perhaps rights bundles are a relatively esoteric construction of complex societies and their attendant legal systems or alternatively, a folk interpretation of rights bundles is early emerging, universal, and a guiding influence on the legal rules.

The single-link and rights bundle frameworks both focus on the nature of the link between person and property and represent competing theories of how owners are related to their property. Thus, we explore ownership by investigating property, owners, and the rules that govern property transfers. By examining the boundaries of the owner–property relationship, it should be possible to shed light on concepts of property more generally. In addition, if certain components in a bundle have a

NEW DIRECTIONS FOR CHILD AND ADOLESCENT DEVELOPMENT • DOI: 10.1002/cd

privileged status and are expected but not strictly necessary, they might constitute a kind of intermediate case between single links and an equally weighted set of components in a bundle. If a single link built up on associations were the only basis for determining owner–property relationships, it would suggest that all property could be conceived of as simply a matter of degree of association to various entities that count as owners. In reality, people's intuitions seem much more structured and nuanced in ways that cannot be modeled by a single link.

What Is Property?

Property (i.e., what can be owned) is one of the most mysterious aspects of ownership. People can identify property when they see it, but they may not have explicit access to the criteria that they employ in identifying property. Economists suggest that property is "created" when a resource is both limited and in demand (Demsetz, 1967), but definitions of property can change over time (e.g., slavery was legal for the majority of human history, but not currently) and from place to place (e.g., it is illegal to own certain animals in Manhattan, but not elsewhere in the United States), which complicates any attempts to define property. Even lawyers, most of whom are required to enroll in a course entitled "Property" in their first year of law school, settle disputes over property without access to any coherent definition of property. Property rules are simply declared by legal systems with vague appeals to overarching principles. Some Property texts provide no definition of property (e.g., Burke, Burkhart, & Helmholz, 2004; Casner, Leach, French, Korngold, & VanderVelde, 2004), while others are surprisingly vague, such as "property consists of anything that can be used, physically or mentally, so as to provide value of some kind" (DeLong, 1997, p. 26), or provide vague references to John Locke (for a review of philosophical theories of ownership and property, see Buckle, 1991). Some legal theorists have acknowledged this shortcoming. One textbook author notes, "What is property? Nearly every first-year property course begins and ends with this query. The instructor never answers the question, but in the asking, and in the quest for meaning, every student gains some glimpse of the variety of possible answers. The question is unanswerable because the meaning of the chameleon-like word property constantly changes in time and space" (Cribbet, 1986, p. 1).

Any meaningful theory of property must account for changes in the definition of property over time and across cultures, creating a major challenge for theorists. Our approach, drawing on elements of both economics and law, focuses on scarcity and access. Property can be considered as created when an individual or group can demonstrate the ability to use and restrict access to a given physical or cognitive resource (Demsetz, 1967). This resource then remains property until an individual or group with practical or legal influence declares the resource to be nonproperty and then acts to enforce this declaration. For example, people were property until governments were committed to the ideal of abolishing slavery. Conversely, powerful groups or individuals can create property by managing access to resources that need not be scarce, even if these manipulations are not undertaken through changes in custom or law. For example, public space like a playground might "belong" to a street gang if they thoroughly restrict the public's use of the area.

To evaluate this view, we first need to determine what is and is not currently considered to be property. Because children are less indoctrinated with cultural and historical information, we chose to approach this task by examining children's intuitions about property and by comparing those intuitions with those of adults. Our goal was to identify rough boundaries for defining property that might apply to a variety of culture and historical settings. We (Noles, Keil, & Bloom, 2009) presented five-, eight-, and ten-year-olds, and adults with items that represented two broad sets of features that might be diagnostic in identifying property. The first set concerned the kinds of things that could be owned. Children were presented with animals, inorganic natural kinds, artifacts, events (e.g., a party), and knowledge (e.g., an original story). The second set was pragmatic, consisting of items that were manipulated for amount, pitting an all-inclusive value (e.g., all the computers in the world) against a single unit (e.g., a single computer), and time (e.g., varying the persistence of objects, such as a cube of ice that will melt in five minutes or a beetle that lives for seventy-five years). Each participant also received three items focusing on humans as property. These target items were presented in owner–object pairs, including adult owners—work by Blake and Harris (2009) indicates that children may not extend full property rights to child owners—and a target item. All items were presented in the following manner: "Can [adult owner name] own a [target item]?"

Adults and children employed similar heuristics when identifying property. Participants endorsed discrete items and rejected items that crossed pragmatic boundaries (e.g., rejecting all-inclusive values), while differences that did not ostensibly restrict ownership (i.e., time) were ignored. A similar boundary was apparent across kinds of potential property. Participants determined that natural kinds, artifacts, and privileged information (e.g., original stories and ideas) were property, but events, common knowledge (e.g., knowing a building's location), and other humans were not identified as property. Friedman, Neary, Defeyter, and Malcolm (this volume) reported similar findings but found that children's conclusions were influenced by historical attributes of objects (e.g., some natural kinds are not assumed to be owned unless an individual previously possessed it). These data suggest that concepts of property emerge early and remain largely consistent throughout development. Further investigation is necessary to determine how these basic boundaries interact with the actions and intentions of individuals and social groups to influence definitions of property; however, it does seem that the scarcity-access approach (Demsetz, 1967) is supported.

Who or What Are Owners?

Having explored concepts of property, another way of understanding how owners relate to their property is to investigate concepts of "owners." In *The Wealth of Nations*, Adam Smith (1776/1977) said, "Nobody ever saw a dog make a fair and deliberate exchange of one bone for another with another dog. Nobody ever saw one animal by its gestures and natural cries signify to another, this is mine, that is yours; I am willing to give this for that." To examine this claim empirically, we presented children, including six-, eight-, and ten-year-olds, and adults with a wide range of entities, such as humans across a developmental continuum (e.g., babies, teens, adults, etc.), "atypical" humans (e.g., individuals who were asleep, unable to move, etc.), a variety of nonhuman animals (e.g., insects, dogs, monkeys, etc.), and artifacts. As in our investigation of property, participants were presented with owner–object pairs (e.g., "Can a dog own a fax?"). The experiments in this investigation differed in that the qualities of the owners were manipulated, rather than the property. Our results indicate that both children and adults employ a "humans only" criterion for identifying owners. However, children eight and under were more restrictive than adults, systematically rejecting that atypical humans can be owners. Examining the atypical human items more closely revealed that young children endorsed low IQ individuals as owners, but they determined that individuals who were paralyzed, insensitive to their surroundings (i.e., they cannot see, hear, or speak), comatose, or asleep could not own property (Noles, Keil, & Bloom, under review).

It was particularly surprising that individuals who were simply asleep were not identified as owners. Research on children's understanding of agency (e.g., Barrett & Behne, 2005) indicates that even our youngest participants should understand states such as sleep, wakefulness, and even death quite well. It therefore seems that one or two conceptual changes may be at work. First, adults and young children may differ in the way that they conceptualize ownership links. Returning for a moment to the two theories of ownership discussed, it is possible that children may view ownership as a strict single link between owner and property, in contrast to adults who may employ a rights bundle formulation. If children do view ownership as a single link, then the inability to exercise any single property right (e.g., if an owner cannot use their property) may indicate a lack of ownership, whereas adults, employing rights bundle representations, continue to entertain the possibility that the entity could be an owner. Therefore, Hohfeld (1913) may have been accurate in positing that ownership historically shifted from a single-link representation to a rights bundle representation, and it is possible that children experience a developmental version of this evolution over the course of childhood. A second, and not necessarily exclusive, possibility is that adults and children conceptualize the owner–property relationship in different ways. Specifically, adults may construe ownership as a passive and persistent social process involving both owners (who protect their privileged access to property) and nonowners (who observe and maintain owner–property links), whereas children may infer that ownership is an active *psychological* endeavor. For example, if children construe ownership as a solitary, active process (i.e., something that an owner *does*), then they may infer that owner–property links may not be formed or maintained by someone who cannot act intentionally, as is the case with individuals who are asleep or otherwise restricted in their actions. Similarly, children may underrepresent the contributions of the social network around them, failing to understand that both owners and the surrounding social context maintain property rights through various social institutions and practices. For adults, ownership seems to be a passive process because, except in certain specific legal situations (e.g., taxation), nothing short of an intentional transfer or destruction can break the connection between owner and property. Furthermore, for adults, ownership seems to be social because it confers a privileged status between an owner and their property that is observed and maintained by both owners and nonowners according to local legal and moral precedents. A failure to represent either of these elements may cause children to represent both owners and ownership differently than adults in certain situations. In contrast to concepts of property, concepts of owners may show some differences between children and adults. The pattern of responses exhibited by young children indicates that, unlike concepts of property, owner concepts may take time and experience to fully develop. The status of ownership as a social construct is discussed in detail by Kalish and Anderson (this volume).

What Are the Rules That Govern Property Transfer?

In addition to notions of owners and property, another critical component of understanding ownership concerns an understanding of principles governing property transfer. Recent studies indicate that adults (Friedman, 2008) and children (Friedman & Neary, 2008) use the same heuristic, first possession, to identify the owners of objects in ambiguous situations. However, although children appear to grasp this principle at an early age, they do not appear to master the rules that govern property transfers until much later in development. Anecdotal evidence suggests that many parents leave a store only to discover on the ride home that their young child has mysteriously acquired candy or a new toy that no one actually purchased. In very young children, this sort of behavior can only be categorized as a mistake, and yet older children also exhibit behaviors that baffle parents and teachers. For example, a child might trade a portable video game system for a particularly attractive sticker. Although this behavior may result from difficulties calculating value, some of these occurrences may also be attributable to children's incomplete understanding of property transfers. This hypothesis is supported by several empirical investigations. For example, both Blake and Harris (2009) and Friedman and Neary (2008) found that children under the age of four exhibited a "first possessor" bias when presented with a very familiar property transfer (i.e., gift-giving at a birthday party), but that young children inferred that ownership was conserved by gift-givers, even when the property transfer was explicit in less familiar scenarios (e.g., see Friedman & Neary, 2008). These findings mirror previous findings with older children obtained by Hook (1993), who found a similar bias in children eight and younger, and concluded that children treated giving as lending, rather than as a permanent property transfer. In contrast, Kim and Kalish (2009) found that young children often correctly attribute property rights to owners following a property transfer when resolving conflicts between owners and nonowners.

There are some inconsistencies between these studies. For example, Hook posits that this biased behavior extends to eight-year-olds, while Blake and Harris (2009) indicate that these biases are attenuated at age five. The most obvious difference between the two studies is that Blake and Harris employed a birthday party vignette, while the property transfers employed by Hook (1993) were neutral. It seems possible that the familiar gift-giving script employed by Blake and Harris (2009), a birthday party, may have conferred some advantage on their participants. However, when Kim and Kalish (2009) queried four- and five-year-old participants about property rights employing a more neutral scenario, they reported that children reliably identified owners both before and after property transfers, despite using perhaps the most complex procedure of these three studies (i.e., presenting more queries about more topics per scenario than previous investigations).

Property transfers represent an emerging area in the study of ownership. In some investigations, children exhibit difficulties attributing ownership following transfers, suggesting that examining the contrasts between transfers and nontransfers might help us to understand how adults and children differ in their ownership attributions. To expand upon previous findings and explore these inconsistencies, we (Noles & Keil, under review) presented children ages eight and ten, and adults with vignettes depicting a wide variety of property transfers, including nontransfers (e.g., borrowing), transfers (e.g., selling), and losses (e.g., theft). These property transfers were also presented in two contexts, including a narrative context (e.g., "Tom let Alex borrow his skateboard for a week.") and a first-person context (e.g., "I [the experimenter] let you borrow this [a low-value object] for a week."). Participants were asked to indicate the owner of the object at the end of each trial and their responses were collapsed across transfer type.

NEW DIRECTIONS FOR CHILD AND ADOLESCENT DEVELOPMENT • DOI: 10.1002/cd

When presented with the narrative context items, both age groups of children provided response patterns similar to adults with respect to non-transfers and losses.[1] However, eight-year-olds demonstrated a strong first-possessor bias, indicating that the initial owner of an object continued to own the property even after explicitly giving or selling the object to someone else, when presented with transfers. Although these data align with Hook's (1993) early findings, the behavior of eight-year-olds in this study does not align with the commonplace intuition that children *do* understand property transfers. When someone hands her child a toy or some food, the child does not act as if they are confused, and certainly children celebrating their birthday understand that they have acquired new possessions. Our first-person context study was designed to address this apparent disconnect between children's responses in ownership studies and common intuitions about children's behavior. The first-person context only differed from that narrative context in that the transfers, nontransfers, and losses were directed from the experimenter to the child, as opposed to occurring between two story characters, and the items from the narrative were replaced with a variety of low-value actual items (e.g., wooden dowels, wall anchors, etc.).

Presenting the items in a first-person context greatly attenuated the first-possessor bias (Noles & Keil, under review), an effect that we attribute to the action of an age-neutral self-serving bias whose presence is implicated by a significant change in responses to theft items. Specifically, in the narrative context, all age groups almost unanimously indicate that the owner, and not the thief, continues to own stolen property, while in the first-person context, approximately 30 percent of participants—distributed equally across age groups—indicate that the thief owns the property after a theft (i.e., when the subject is described as the thief, the theft is much more likely to be identified as a property transfer).

Young children exhibit a strong first-possessor bias, perhaps stemming from early ownership heuristics (see Friedman & Neary, 2008). When presented with even the most explicit of property transfers, children often conserve ownership, and perhaps property rights, with an object's first owner. This finding has been discovered and reliably replicated across several age groups. However, the first-possessor bias may be attenuated or eliminated in at least two ways. First, the findings of Blake and Harris (2009), Kim and Kalish (2009), and Neary and Friedman (2008) suggest that activating well-learned social scripts (e.g., a birthday party) or querying children on property rights, rather than ownership,

---

[1]There was one exception, which was the "discard" item in the loss category. Adults interpreted discarding (i.e., intentionally throwing an item into the garbage) as a property transfer; eight-year-olds and, to a lesser degree, ten-year-olds interpreted this behavior as a nontransfer, conserving ownership with the first possessor.

NEW DIRECTIONS FOR CHILD AND ADOLESCENT DEVELOPMENT • DOI: 10.1002/cd

may attenuate the first-possessor bias in young children. Second, situational factors may also contribute to the attenuation of this bias, as in the first-person context discussed previously (Noles & Keil, under review). Although children's insistence on conserving ownership may appear to be a simple mistake, we hypothesize that this behavior is both complex and adaptive. Specifically, a first-possessor bias may lead children to assume a conservative stance when *observing* property transfers among other people, while assuming a very liberal stance when *receiving* property transfers. This cross-context balancing act may allow children to be conservative in a manner that reduces accidental violations of property rights, while allowing the child to be maximally receptive to property transfers in their direction. Further studies are needed to fully understand children's concepts of property transfers and the role of first-possessor biases.

Conclusions

Understanding the development of ownership behaviors is a critical component of understanding the cognitions that underlie ownership and economic behaviors. Although some aspects of ownership are early emerging, other aspects take time and experience to fully develop. Furthermore, the patterns of development vary considerably. Concepts of property appear early and do not change drastically over the course of development, whereas concepts of owners and property rights appear to grow and change until early adolescence and perhaps beyond.

Humans in all societies live and develop in a complex and multilayered web of relationships among people and property. Ownership plays an important role in individuals' lives regardless of age or culture. Indeed, concepts of property and possession are even salient to nonhumans (see Brosnan, this volume). The cognitive operations that drive human ownership inferences and behaviors, however, remain an important, understudied research topic. New studies are rapidly appearing examining social, cognitive, and developmental aspects of ownership, but additional interdisciplinary studies are especially needed to explore ownership within the contexts of conceptual development, social cognition, and culture. Ownership is not a concept reserved for those in positions of power, privilege, or wealth. It is a wonderfully democratic concept even as the kinds of things owned may vary radically across various groups. All of us somehow come to master the complex web of ownership relations that saturate all cultures. The challenge lies in understanding how this comes about through the course of development in an apparently effortless manner.

References

Barrett, H. C., & Behne, T. (2005). Children's understanding of death as the cessation of agency: A test using sleep versus death. *Cognition, 96,* 93–108.

Belk, R. W. (1988). Possessions and the extended self. *Journal of Consumer Research, 15*, 139–168.

Blake, P. R., & Harris, P. L. (2009). Children's understanding of ownership transfer. *Cognitive Development, 24*, 133–145.

Blake, P. R., & Harris, P. L. (2011). Early representations of ownership. In H. Ross & O. Friedman (Eds.), *Origins of ownership of property. New Directions for Child and Adolescent Development, 132*, 39–52.

Brosnan, S. F. (2011). Property in nonhuman primates. In H. Ross & O. Friedman (Eds.), *Origins of ownership of property. New Directions for Child and Adolescent Development, 132*, 9–22.

Buckle, S. (1991). *Natural law and the theory of property: Grotius to Hume*. New York, NY: Oxford University Press.

Burke, B., Burkhart, A. M., & Helmholz, R. H. (2004). *Fundamentals of property law* (2nd ed.). Newark, NJ: Matthew Bender & Company.

Casner, A. J., Leach, W. B., French, S. F., Korngold, G., & VanderVelde, L. (2004). *Cases and text on property* (5th ed.). New York, NY: Aspen Publishers.

Cram, F., & Paton, H. (1993). Personal possessions and self-identity: The experiences of elderly women in three residential settings. *Australian Journal on Ageing, 12*, 19–24.

Cribbet, J. E. (1986). Concepts in transition: The search for a new definition of property. *The University of Illinois Law Review, 1*, 1–42.

DeLong, J. V. (1997). *Property matters*. New York, NY: The Free Press.

Demsetz, H. (1967). Toward a theory of property rights. *American Economic Review, 62*, 347–359.

Dittmar, H. (1991). Meanings of material possessions as reflections of identity: Gender and social-material position in society. *Journal of Social Behavior and Personality, 6*, 165–186.

Dittmar, H. (1992). *The social psychology of material possessions*. New York, NY: St. Martin's Press.

Dittmar, H. (1994). Material possessions as stereotypes: Material images of different socio-economic groups. *Journal of Economic Psychology, 15*, 561–585.

Fasig, L. G. (2000). Toddlers' understanding of ownership: Implications for self-concept development. *Social Development, 9*, 370–382.

Frank, R. H. (2000). *Luxury fever: Money and happiness in an era of excess*. Princeton, NJ: Princeton University Press.

Friedman, O. (2008). First possession: An assumption guiding inferences about who owns what. *Psychonomic Bulletin & Review, 15*, 290–295.

Friedman, O., & Neary, K. R. (2008). Determining who owns what: Do children infer ownership from first possession? *Cognition, 107*, 829–849.

Friedman, O., Neary, K. R., Defeyter, M. A., & Malcolm, S. L. (2011). Ownership and object history. In H. Ross & O. Friedman (Eds.), *Origins of ownership of property. New Directions for Child and Adolescent Development, 132*, 79–89.

Furby, L. (1991). Understanding the psychology of possession and ownership: A personal memoir and an appraisal of our progress. *Journal of Social Behavior and Personality, 6*, 457–463.

Harbaugh, W. T., Krause, K., & Berry, T. R. (2001). GARP for kids: On the development of rational choice behavior. *The American Economic Review, 91*, 1539–1545.

Harbaugh, W. T., Krause, K., & Vesterlund, L. (2001). Are adults better behaved than children? Age, experience, and the endowment effect. *Economic Letters, 70*, 175–181.

Hay, D. F., & Ross, H. S. (1982). The social nature of early conflict. *Child Development, 53*, 105–113.

Hohfeld, W. H. (1913). Some fundamental legal conceptions as applied to judicial reasoning. *Yale Law Journal, 23*, 16–59.

Hohfeld, W. H. (1917). Fundamental legal conceptions as applied to judicial reasoning. *Yale Law Journal, 26,* 710–770.

Hook, J. (1993). Judgments about the right to property from preschool to adulthood. *Law and Human Behavior, 17,* 135–146.

Kahneman, D., Knetsch, J. L., & Thaler, R. H. (1990). Experimental tests of the endowment effect and the Coase theorem. *The Journal of Political Economy, 98,* 1325–1348.

Kalish, C. W., & Anderson, C. D. (2011). Ownership as a social status. In H. Ross & O. Friedman (Eds.), *Origins of ownership of property. New Directions for Child and Adolescent Development, 132,* 65–77.

Kamptner, N. L. (1991). Personal possessions and their meanings: A life span perspective. *Journal of Social Behavior and Personality, 6,* 209–228.

Kim, S., & Kalish, C.W. (2009). Children's ascriptions of property rights with changes of ownership. *Cognitive Development, 24,* 322–336.

Noles, N. S., & Keil, F. C. (under review). Two biases affect children's inferences of ownership across transfers of property.

Noles, N. S., Keil, F. C., & Bloom, P. (2009, April). *Categorical and pragmatic boundaries guide children and adults in identifying property.* Poster presented at the bi-annual meeting of the Society for Research in Child Development, Denver, CO.

Noles, N. S., Keil, F. C., & Bloom, P. (under review). Possession attribution asymmetries: Context influences children's attributions of ownership.

Prentice, D. A. (1987). Psychological correspondence of possessions, attitudes, and values. *Journal of Personality and Social Psychology, 53,* 993–1003.

Rochat, P. (2011). Possession and morality in early development. In H. Ross & O. Friedman (Eds.), *Origins of ownership of property. New Directions for Child and Adolescent Development, 132,* 23–38.

Ross, H., Conant, C., & Vickar, M. (2011). Property rights and the resolution of social conflict. In H. Ross & O. Friedman (Eds.), *Origins of ownership of property. New Directions for Child and Adolescent Development, 132,* 53–64.

Ross, H. S. (1996). Negotiating principles of entitlement in sibling property disputes. *Developmental Psychology, 32,* 90–101.

Rudmin, F. W. (1990). The economic psychology of Leon Litwinski (1887–1969): A program of cognitive research on possession and property. *Journal of Economic Psychology, 11,* 307–339.

Rudmin, F. W. (1991). "To own is to be perceived to own": A social cognitive look at the ownership of property. *Journal of Social Behavior and Personality, 6,* 85–104.

Smith, A. (1977). *An inquiry into the nature and causes of the wealth of nations* (E. Cannan, Ed.). Chicago, IL: University of Chicago Press. (Original work published 1776).

Snare, F. (1972). The concept of property. *American Philosophical Quarterly, 9,* 200–206.

Thaler, R. (1980). Toward a positive theory of consumer choice. *Journal of Economic Behavior and Organization, 1,* 39–60.

NICHOLAUS S. NOLES *is a postdoctoral fellow in the Psychology Department at The University of Michigan. E-mail: nsnoles@umich.edu; webpage: sitemaker.umich.edu/noles.*

FRANK C. KEIL *is a professor of psychology and linguistics at Yale University, New Haven, Connecticut. E-mail: frank.keil@yale.edu; webpage: www.yale .edu/cogdevlab.*

NEW DIRECTIONS FOR CHILD AND ADOLESCENT DEVELOPMENT • DOI: 10.1002/cd

INDEX

ings in the inevitable dilemmas young people face when required to balance between normative expectations and individual aspirations. *ISBN 978-04709-31127*

CAD129   *Children's Moral Emotions and Moral Cognition: Developmental and Educational Perspectives*
Brigitte Latzko, Tina Malti
Children's emerging morality involves the development of moral emotions and moral cognition. Developmental research suggests that emotions play an important role in dealing with moral conflict situations, and they help children differentiate moral concepts from other social judgments. However, emotions and their role in moral cognition and moral behavior have yet to be addressed systematically in empirical research. In this volume, the authors show how integrative developmental research on children's moral emotions and moral cognition can help us understand how children's morality evolves. As both moral emotions and moral cognition are related to children's moral, prosocial behavior, as well as to their immoral, aggressive behavior, studying how moral emotions and moral cognition interact is not only of conceptual significance to developmental researchers, but also of practical importance to educators. A central premise of the volume is that moral emotions interact with moral cognition in different ways across development. An integrative developmental perspective on moral emotions and moral cognition thus offers an important conceptual framework for understanding children's emerging morality and designing developmentally sensitive moral intervention strategies. The authors summarize the empirical literature linking moral emotions to moral cognition and discuss promising conceptual avenues and methodological approaches to study children's moral emotions and moral cognition. They also provide examples illustrating how the principles of integrative moral education can be applied in educational practice.
ISBN 978-04709-03889

CAD128   *Focus on Gender: Parent and Child Contributions to the Socialization of Emotional Competence*
Amy Kennedy Root, Susanne A. Denham, Editors
Gender's influence on human development is all encompassing. In fact, "Virtually all of human functioning has a gendered cast—appearance, mannerisms, communication, temperament, activities at home and outside, aspirations, and values" (Ruble, Martin, & Berenbaum, 2006, p. 858).
     In short, gender impacts growth in a multitude of developmental domains, including the development of emotion and emotional competence. Although emotions are, in part, biological, the meanings of emotions and appropriateness of emotional expression are socialized. In the early years of life, socialization primarily takes place via interactions within the family, and characteristics of both parents and children may affect the process of emotion socialization. Gender is one critically important moderator of what and how children learn about emotion because culture determines the appropriateness of emotional displays for males and females.
     The goal of this sourcebook is to provide a comprehensive volume addressing what we see as the critical issues in the study of gender, emotion socialization, and the development of emotional competence. Each of the chapters provides evidence for the pervasive role that gender plays in emotional development and provides a framework to better understand the development of emotion in boys and girls.
ISBN 978-04706-47868

CAD127   *Social Anxiety in Childhood: Bridging Developmental and Clinical Perspectives*
Heidi Gazelle, Kenneth H. Rubin, Editors
Social anxiety in childhood is the focus of research in three psychological research traditions: developmental studies emphasizing dispositional constructs such as behavioral inhibition and its biological substrates; developmental investigations emphasizing affective-behavioral characteristics (anxious solitude/withdrawal) and their parent–child and peerrelational precursors and moderators; and clinical investigations of social anxiety disorder (also known as social phobia) emphasizing a variety of etiological factors, diagnosis, and treatment. In this volume, we review and identify gaps in extant evidence that permit (or impede) researchers from the three traditions to translate their core definitional constructs in ways that would facilitate the use of one another's research. Intimately connected to this translation of constructs is a discussion of the conceptualization of core states (anxiety, wariness, solitude) and their manifestations across childhood, as well as corresponding methodologies. Extant research is analyzed from an integrative, overarching framework of developmental psychopathology in which children's adjustment is conceptualized as multiply determined such that children who share certain risks may display diverse adjustment over time (multifinality) and children with diverse risks may develop shared adaptational difficulties over time (equifinality). Finally, key themes for future integrative research are identified and implications for preventative and early intervention in childhood social anxiety are discussed.
ISBN 978-04706-18059

CAD126   **Siblings as Agents of Socialization**
Laurie Kramer, Katherine J. Conger, Editors
Siblings have considerable influence on children's development, yet most human development research has neglected the investigation of sibling socialization in favor of a focus on parental socialization. This volume uses a family systems framework to examine the ways in which siblings contribute uniquely to one another's social and emotional development. The groundbreaking lines of research in this volume address mechanisms by which children are influenced by their sisters and brothers, ways in which these processes of sibling socialization are similar to and different from those with parents, and conditions under which sibling socialization has positive versus negative impact on individual development. Throughout this volume, attention is devoted to contextual factors that moderate sibling influences, such as family structure, life course events, ethnicity and culture, gender, and demographic indicators.
ISBN 978-04706-14594

CAD125   **Evidentiality: A Window Into Language and Cognitive Development**
Stanka A. Fitneva, Tomoko Matsui, Editors
Much recent research investigates children's understanding of the sources of human knowledge and the relation of this understanding to socio-cognitive development. This volume of *New Directions for Child and Adolescent Development* highlights new research in this area that focuses on evidentials: word affixes and sentence particles that indicate the speaker's source of knowledge—for example, perception, inference, or hearsay. Evidentials are a feature of about a quarter of the languages in the world and have a variety of interesting characteristics. For example, in contrast to lexical alternatives familiar from English, such as "I saw," they are extremely frequent. The volume brings together scholars pioneering research on evidentiality

in Bulgarian, Japanese, Tibetan, and Turkish. Their contributions to this volume provide a glimpse at the diversity of evidential systems around the globe while examining a number of provocative questions: How do evidentials mediate children's acquisition of knowledge from others' testimony? What is the relation between grammaticalized and lexical expressions of source of knowledge? Does the acquisition of an evidential system boost source monitoring and inferential skills? The volume is a compelling illustration of the relevance of evidentiality to broadening our understanding of development in many domains, including theory of mind, memory, and knowledge acquisition.
ISBN 978-04705-69658

CAD124   **Coping and the Development of Regulation**
Ellen A. Skinner, Melanie J. Zimmer-Gembeck, Editors
A developmental conceptualization that emphasizes coping as regulation under stress opens the way to explore synergies between coping and regulatory processes, including self-regulation; behavioral, emotion, attention, and action regulation; ego control; self-control; compliance; and volition. This volume, with chapters written by experts on the development of regulation and coping during childhood and adolescence, is the first to explore these synergies. The volume is geared toward researchers working in the broad areas of regulation, coping, stress, adversity, and resilience. For regulation researchers, it offers opportunities to focus on age-graded changes in how these processes function under stress and to consider multiple targets of regulation simultaneously—emotion, attention, behavior—that typically are examined in isolation. For researchers interested in coping, this volume offers invigorating theoretical and operational ideas. For researchers studying stress, adversity, and resilience, the volume highlights coping as one pathway through which exposure to adversity shapes children's long-term development. The authors also address cross-cutting developmental themes, such as the role of stress, coping, and social relationships in the successive integration of regulatory subsystems, the emergence of autonomous regulation, and the progressive construction of the kinds of regulatory resources and routines that allow flexible constructive coping under successively higher levels of stress and adversity. All chapters emphasize the importance of integrative multilevel perspectives in bringing together work on the neurobiology of stress, temperament, attachment, regulation, personal resources, relationships, stress exposure, and social contexts in studying processes of coping, adversity, and resilience.
ISBN 978-04705-31372

CAD 123   **Social Interaction and the Development of Executive Function**
Charlie Lewis, Jeremy I. M. Carpendale, Editors
Executive function consists of higher cognitive skills that are involved in the control of thought, action, and emotion. It has been linked to neural systems involving the prefrontal cortex, but a full definition of the term has remained elusive partly because it includes such a complex set of cognitive processes. Relatively little is known about the processes that promote development of executive function, and how it is linked to children's social behavior. The key factor examined by the chapters in this issue is the role of social interaction, and the chapters take an increasingly broad perspective. Two end pieces introduce the topic as a whole (Chapter 1) and present an integrative commentary on the articles (Chapter 6) in an attempt to stress the social origins of executive function, in contrast to many contemporary cognitive approach-

es. The empirical contributions in between examine the roles of parental scaffolding of young preschoolers (Chapter 2), the links between maternal education and conversational support (Chapter 3), how such family background factors and social skills extend into adolescence (Chapter 4), and wider cultural influences (Chapter 5) on development of executive skills. This volume is aimed at a broad range of developmental researchers and practitioners interested in the influences of family background and interactions as well as educational and cultural processes on development of the child's self-control and social understanding. Such relationships have wide implications for many aspects of the lives of children and adolescents.
ISBN 978-04704-89017

CAD 122   ***Core Competencies to Prevent Problem Behaviors and Promote Positive Youth Development***
Nancy G. Guerra, Catherine P. Bradshaw, Editors
Adolescence generally is considered a time of experimentation and increased involvement in risk or problem behaviors, including early school leaving, violence, substance use, and high-risk sexual behavior. In this volume, the authors show how individual competencies linked to well-being can reduce youth involvement in these risk behaviors. Five core competencies are emphasized: a positive sense of self, self-control, decision-making skills, a moral system of belief, and prosocial connectedness. A central premise of this volume is that high levels of the core competencies provide a marker for positive youth development, whereas low levels increase the likelihood of adolescent risk behavior. The authors summarize the empirical literature linking these competencies to each risk behavior, providing examples from developmental and prevention research. They highlight programs and policies in the United States and internationally that have changed one or more dimensions of the core competencies through efforts designed to build individual skills, strengthen relationships, and enhance opportunities and supports across multiple developmental contexts.
ISBN 978-04704-42166

CAD 121   ***Beyond the Family: Contexts of Immigrant Children's Development***
Hirokazu Yoshikawa, Niobe Way, Editors
Immigration in the United States has become a central focus of policy and public concern in the first decade of the 21st century. This volume aims to broaden developmental research on children and youth in immigrant families. Much of the research on immigrant children and youth concentrates on family characteristics such as parenting, demographic, or human capital features. In this volume, we consider the developmental consequences for immigrant youth of broader contexts such as social networks, peer discrimination in school and out-of-school settings, legal contexts, and access to institutional resources. Chapters answer questions such as: How do experiences of discrimination affect the lives of immigrant youth? How do social networks of immigrant families influence children's learning? How do immigrant parents' citizenship status influence family life and their children's development? In examining factors as disparate as discrimination based on physical appearance, informal adult helpers, and access to drivers' licenses, these chapters serve to enrich our notions of how culture and context shape human development, as well as inform practice and public policy affecting immigrant families.
ISBN 978-04704-17300

NEW DIRECTIONS FOR CHILD AND ADOLESCENT DEVELOPMENT
ORDER FORM SUBSCRIPTION AND SINGLE ISSUES

DISCOUNTED BACK ISSUES:

Use this form to receive 20% off all back issues of *New Directions for Child and Adolescent Development*. All single issues priced at **$23.20** (normally $29.00)

TITLE	ISSUE NO.	ISBN
_____	_____	_____
_____	_____	_____
_____	_____	_____

Call 888-378-2537 or see mailing instructions below. When calling, mention the promotional code JBNND to receive your discount. For a complete list of issues, please visit www.josseybass.com/go/ndcad

SUBSCRIPTIONS: (1 YEAR, 4 ISSUES)

☐ New Order   ☐ Renewal

U.S.	☐ Individual: $89	☐ Institutional: $315
CANADA/MEXICO	☐ Individual: $89	☐ Institutional: $355
ALL OTHERS	☐ Individual: $113	☐ Institutional: $389

Call 888-378-2537 or see mailing and pricing instructions below.
Online subscriptions are available at www.onlinelibrary.wiley.com

ORDER TOTALS:

Issue / Subscription Amount: $ _____

Shipping Amount: $ _____
(for single issues only – subscription prices include shipping)

Total Amount: $ _____

SHIPPING CHARGES:	
First Item	$5.00
Each Add'l Item	$3.00

(No sales tax for U.S. subscriptions. Canadian residents, add GST for subscription orders. Individual rate subscriptions must be paid by personal check or credit card. Individual rate subscriptions may not be resold as library copies.)

BILLING & SHIPPING INFORMATION:

☐ **PAYMENT ENCLOSED:** *(U.S. check or money order only. All payments must be in U.S. dollars.)*

☐ **CREDIT CARD:** ☐ VISA ☐ MC ☐ AMEX

Card number _____Exp. Date_____

Card Holder Name_____Card Issue # _____

Signature _____Day Phone_____

☐ **BILL ME:** *(U.S. institutional orders only. Purchase order required.)*

Purchase order # _____
Federal Tax ID 13559302 • GST 89102-8052

Name_____

Address_____

Phone_____ E-mail_____

Copy or detach page and send to: **John Wiley & Sons, PTSC, 5th Floor**
989 Market Street, San Francisco, CA 94103-1741

Order Form can also be faxed to: **888-481-2665**

PROMO JBNND